Cataclysm 90 BC

Cataclysm 90 BC

The Forgotten War That Almost Destroyed Rome

Philip Matyszak

Pen & Sword
MILITARY

First published in Great Britain in 2014
and republished in this format in 2021 by
Pen & Sword Military
an imprint of
Pen & Sword Books Ltd
Yorkshire – Philadelphia

Copyright © Philip Matyszak 2014, 2021

ISBN 978 1 39908 518 2

The right of Philip Matyszak to be identified as the Author of this
Work has been asserted by him in accordance with the Copyright,
Designs and Patents Act 1988.

A CIP catalogue record for this book is available from the British Library

All rights reserved. No part of this book may be reproduced or
transmitted in any form or by any means, electronic or mechanical
including photocopying, recording or by any information storage and
retrieval system, without permission from the Publisher in writing.

Typeset in Ehrhardt by Mac Style Ltd
Printed in the UK by CPI Group (UK) Ltd, Croydon, CR0 4YY

Pen & Sword Books Limited incorporates the imprints of Atlas,
Archaeology, Aviation, Discovery, Family History, Fiction, History,
Maritime, Military, Military Classics, Politics, Select, Transport, True
Crime, Air World, Frontline Publishing, Leo Cooper, Remember When,
Seaforth Publishing, The Praetorian Press, Wharncliffe Local History,
Wharncliffe Transport, Wharncliffe True Crime and White Owl.

For a complete list of Pen & Sword titles please contact

PEN & SWORD BOOKS LIMITED
47 Church Street, Barnsley, South Yorkshire, S70 2AS, England
E-mail: enquiries@pen-and-sword.co.uk
Website: www.pen-and-sword.co.uk

Or
PEN AND SWORD BOOKS
1950 Lawrence Rd, Havertown, PA 19083, USA
E-mail: Uspen-and-sword@casematepublishers.com
Website: www.penandswordbooks.com

Contents

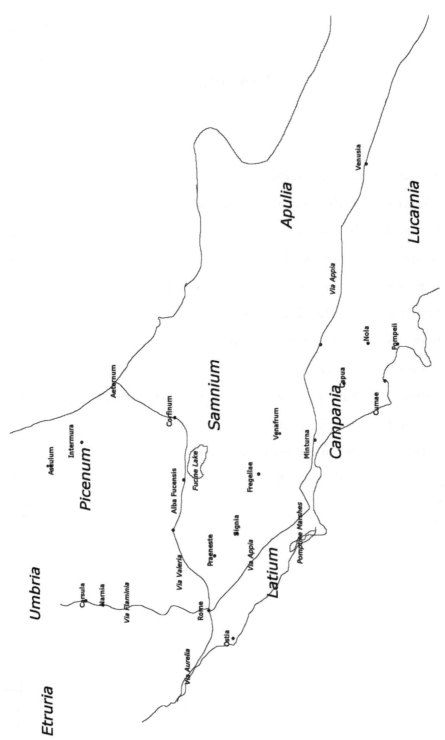

Italy circa 90 BC.

Introduction – the Prophetic Polybius

This book is a study of some very odd events – of nations so desperate to give up their independence that they fought a war against the state that refused to take it; of the Roman Republic losing that war – itself a rarity – then winning by giving their enemies what they wanted. So the only instance in history of the opposite of a war of independence, was also one of the few cases where surrender brought victory to the losing side. It is also a study of how one war can create the conditions for the next and then merge almost seamlessly into it. In such topsy-turvy circumstances it is appropriate to start with a short text of whatever is the opposite of history. This was written by Polybius, the Greek diplomat and soldier, who describes – pretty accurately – events as they happened between thirty and one hundred years in his future.

> Aristocracy by its very nature degenerates into oligarchy. Then the common people become infuriated with this government and take revenge on it for its unjust rule. So we get the development of democracy. In due course the permissiveness and lawlessness of this type of government degenerates into mob-rule, and the cycle is complete.
>
> Polybius, *Histories* 6.3

Thus Polybius saw societies as revolving through six stages – from anarchy to monarchy, through monarchy to tyranny, from tyranny to aristocracy, from aristocracy to oligarchy, and from oligarchy to democracy. Then from democracy to anarchy and round and around again. Writing in the late second century BC, at a time when Rome was the dominant power in the Mediterranean, Polybius believed that one of the reasons for Rome's success was the stability of the political system. This, he opined, combined the best parts of the three best forms of government. Thus:

If one focussed on the power of the consuls, the constitution seemed completely monarchical and biased towards royalty. Again, if one concentrated on the senate it seemed aristocratic, and when one looked at the power of the common people [Rome] clearly appeared to be a democracy.

Polybius, *Histories* 6.11

The consuls provided the monarchical element, but they were prevented from becoming tyrants by the senate, which represented the aristocratic element. The senate was prevented from becoming oligarchical by the people, whose democracy was prevented from degenerating into mob rule by the monarchical and aristocratic elements, Yet even though this constitution was able to slow the cycle of human governance, Polybius was too cynical (or realistic) to believe that the process could altogether be stopped.

The truth of what I have just said will be quite clear to anyone who pays attention ... each form [of government] naturally arises and develops. One can see where, when, and how the growth, peak, change, and end of each form develops. And I believe that, above all, this formula can be successfully applied to the Roman constitution.

Polybius, *Histories* 6.3

For much of his mini-treatise of the Roman Republic, Polybius lauds the balance of the elements in the Rome of his day. He remarks how the aristocracy competed among each other to be of service to the state, how the consuls were chosen to lead the armies of Rome, and how the Roman people themselves were pious, honourable and public-spirited. Rome was in control of the Mediterranean world, and more importantly, Rome was in control of itself. Yet, in these glory days of the Roman Republic Polybius looked ahead. He saw Rome's government degenerating, the system going out of balance and collapsing into chaos and near-anarchy. In short, he foresaw the century to come.

I think it is pretty clear what is going to happen next. When a state endures great danger and subsequently rises to supremacy and uncontested sovereignty, prosperity will become enduring. Under its influence, lifestyles will become more extravagant and the citizens will compete more fiercely than they should for public office and all that goes with it. For as degeneration begins, the first signs of the change for the worse be the coveting of office and the belief that obscurity is disgraceful.

Polybius, *Histories* 6.67

With the advantage of hindsight, this book will describe the unfolding of the developments that Polybius predicted with such foresight. It will also concentrate on something that Polybius, the soldier and statesman, took so much for granted that he did not bother to describe it – the role of the army.

For when Polybius talks of 'the people' he means the people of the Roman Republic, or of the Greek city-states that he knew. For Polybius the 'people' in these states were not the slaves, the children or the womenfolk. They were not even the voters, though voting was an important function of 'the people'. Above all, the people were the army. In the Greece that Polybius knew, and in the Rome of his day, the army was made up of citizens under arms. Many of these citizens enrolled in the levy at the start of the campaigning season in the expectation that they would go home to their family farms or businesses at the end of the year. When 'the people' of such a state become disaffected, the result is not public demonstrations and the hurling of brickbats, or even rioting, which might be controlled by calling in the army. When the army is the people, things much more substantial than brickbats are thrown, and they are thrown with organized professionalism – and since they are the army, the only thing that can stop them is another army.

The people will take the initiative, firstly when they feel aggrieved by individuals who have shown egregious covetousness, and secondly when they are puffed up by the flattery of those looking to hold office. Then, roused to fury, and their decisions ruled by emotion, they will no longer consent to obey or even to be the equals of their rulers.

Polybius, ibid.

And this is what happened in the early first century. Threatened by the migrating Cimbric hordes, Rome was indeed in great danger. This was overcome by a combination of good fortune and great generalship. However, the state that had overcome this peril was already sick, and the subsequent peace led – as Polybius had predicted a generation before – to vicious competition for public office. The aristocracy of the senate had already begun the slide to oligarchy in Polybius' day, and what was once the most open and upwardly mobile of all ancient societies had become exclusionary and self-interested. This trend continued, and provoked the cataclysmic explosion of 91 BC. Yet, even when Roman backs were to the wall and the survival of the state itself in doubt, things could still get worse.

Polybius saw developments moving only in one direction. Oligarchies do not reform and become aristocracies once more, and the Roman aristocracy obediently followed form. And the people responded on cue. Alienated from a corrupted political process, the people took matters into their own hands. And since the people in question were the toughest, most merciless soldiers in the known world, when 'roused to fury and their decisions ruled by passion' the result was never going to be pretty. By the time the dust had more or less settled in 81 BC, Rome's oligarchical senatorial class had quite literally been more than decimated. What staggered from the wreckage of the Roman constitution had still the habits of the Roman Republic, but the system was irreparably damaged and its leaders traumatized.

> The name will be the fairest of all, a free democracy, but its nature will be changed to the worst thing of all – mob rule.
>
> Polybius, ibid.

After 81 BC Rome constantly tottered on the brink of military anarchy, and in 49 BC it fell off the edge altogether when Caesar led his army across the Rubicon. Assassinations, purges, and civil wars followed thick and fast, until from the chaos was produced Augustus – Rome's first emperor and an undoubted autocrat. The Polybian cycle had come the full circle as its author had predicted. Given the tens of thousands that perished in the process, it is unlikely that Polybius would have taken much satisfaction in bring proven right.

The above analysis is of necessity abbreviated and simplistic, but accurate. It provides a skeleton that this book will flesh out, so that the events of 91–81 BC can be seen not as a series of unrelated convulsions but as the violent resolution of a political process that eventually destroyed the Roman Republic.

Chapter 1

Prelude to Cataclysmic Adjustment

The disaster of 91 BC did not come as a bolt from the blue. The problems facing the Roman state had begun developing soon after the end of Rome's drawn-out war with Hannibal of Carthage (218–201 BC). Two generations later, around 150 BC, the fact that the Roman Republic was dysfunctional was obvious enough for contemporary politicians to be aware of it, though no one was willing or able to take action. Why action was difficult became more apparent in the following decades when the politicians who tried to take it paid with their lives for making the attempt. Thereafter the problem was left unsolved. This was the situation until 91 BC.

History tells us that if no remedy is applied to a situation out of balance, matters will eventually resolve themselves by a process known as cataclysmic adjustment. 'Cataclysmic adjustment' does not actually solve a problem but rather changes the problem into something completely different and usually more severe. For example, if the foundations of a house need repairs that they do not receive, cataclysmic adjustment will eventually transform the problem into that of removing a collapsed house and building another. This is roughly analogous with what happened to the Roman Republic. An ongoing structural problem with the state was not addressed (and according to Polybius, could not be addressed – see introduction), and the result was that the Republic collapsed, to be eventually replaced with a new structure.

The years between 150 and 91 BC tell the story of the failure to resolve Rome's structural problems, and the years 91–81 BC describe how the first stage of the collapse took place. It is fair to argue that before 91 BC the Roman Republic might have been saved. After 81 BC failure was inevitable; cataclysmic adjustment had already begun.

There were many things wrong with the Roman Republic of the late second century, but most of these could be traced to one fundamental problem and one major secondary issue. These were, respectively, the failure of inclusivism and dispossession from the land. If we are to understand what happened in 91 BC it is important to first address these two issues at length.

The fundamental problem was the failure of inclusivism. This itself had two parts. Firstly, after the second Punic War the Roman Republic, originally one of the most open societies in the ancient world, changed its policy of absorbing communities into the Roman citizen body. Instead Rome began to guard the citizenship jealously, creating divisions between those who had the privileges and rights of citizenship and those who wanted them. Secondly, the Roman leadership, also once open and inclusive, fell into the hands of a largely closed community of aristocrats. This community defended its privileges and came increasingly to identify its interests as being those of the Roman state as a whole. That is, the Roman political elite, which until then had seen its duty as service to the state, now increasingly adopted the view that the state existed to serve it. This was a substantial change with far-reaching effects to which we shall return.

With inclusivism, there was once a time when access to the Roman citizen body was extremely easy. Mostly it was a matter of turning up and living in Rome for a while. Rome's 'open door' policy was partly because from its earliest days the city was by necessity expansionist. Rome was founded at the lowest crossing point of the river Tiber. This put it right across an ancient trade route that took salt from the coast to the Italian interior – the via Salaria. Furthermore, the Tiber was the unofficial border between Latium and Etruria. Therefore the settlement of Rome managed to displease both Latins and Etruscans. Legend records that the first act of Romulus when he founded the city was to build a defensive wall – it was going to be needed.

Given unfriendly neighbours and local hill tribes with a penchant for pillage, early Rome had to get big or die. To survive, Rome needed new people, and the city was not fussy about how it acquired them. Volunteers were welcome – be they escaped slaves, disbanded mercenaries, reformed bandits or men escaping their creditors. If not enough volunteers arrived, the Romans were ready, willing and able to go out and recruit new members by force; entire communities were unwillingly conscripted into the citizen body. Rome even conquered Alba Longa from whence legend says the original colonists who settled Rome had come. The people of Alba Longa –

including the aristocratic family of the Julians – were forcibly translocated to Rome.

Eventually, as Rome expanded, lack of space on the seven hills meant that bringing home entire conquered populations along with the booty became unrealistic. Still, the Romans did not stop making citizens out of those they had conquered. A new policy left those defeated by the legions in place, but now as involuntary Romans amid the still-smouldering ruins of homes which they were free to rebuild as extensions of the Roman state, far from the city of Rome.

Recognizing that defeated peoples might harbour hard feelings about recent events, the constitution instituted a special status for them. They became *cives sine suffragio* – citizens without the vote. This made a conquered people sort of probationary Romans, entitled to the legal protection of citizenship, but unable (for example) to vote for the immediate execution of the general who had conquered them. If a community behaved itself – and almost all did – then the vote would come along in a generation or two. By that time the grandsons of the defeated were in the legions, enthusiastically expanding the Roman state yet further and forcibly recruiting yet more members of the Roman citizen body.

This openness worked wonders for Roman expansion – as the emperor Claudius later noted. Faced with objections to his giving citizenship to Gauls of the Senones tribe he replied:

Indeed I know for a fact, that the [noble family of the] Julii came from Alba [Longa], the Coruncanii from Camerium, the Porcii from Tusculum. Without going into detail about the past, new members of the Senate have been brought in from Etruria and Lucania and the whole of Italy. The land of Italy itself was extended to the Alps, just so that that not only individuals but entire countries and tribes could be united under our name...

Our founder Romulus was so wise that he fought as enemies and then hailed as fellow-citizens several nations on the very same day. Strangers have reigned over us. That freedmen's sons should be entrusted with public offices ... was a common practice in the old Republic. But, you say, we have fought against the Senones. Then does this mean that the

Volsci and Aequi [now communities of solid Roman citizens] never stood in battle array against us?

Tacitus, *Annals* 11

What applied to the citizenship in general also applied to the most aristocratic Romans. As Claudius said of the Julians and others, not only was access to the Roman citizenship straightforward (and sometimes not even voluntary), membership of the Roman governing class was also highly accessible. The origins of the Roman aristocracy are here described by the later Roman historian Livy.

It was traditional for those founding a city to assemble a horde of the obscure and lowly-born and then make the fictional claim that these people had 'sprung from the soil'. Following this tradition, Romulus opened a place of refuge at the enclosed space between the two groves of trees that you find as you go down from the Capitol. This became an asylum for an indiscriminate crowd of freedmen and [escaped] slaves looking to better their lot. This influx was the first source of strength for the newly-founded city. Satisfied with this, Romulus took steps to see that this strength was properly directed. He created a hundred senators, either because he felt that number was enough or because the city had only a hundred heads of households.

Livy, *From the Founding of the City* 1.1.18

How much of Livy's early history is factual is hotly disputed by academics. Yet just as there is little doubt that the original citizens of Rome were as unsavoury a bunch of riff-raff as any between Sicily and the Alps, the Romans were equally undiscriminating about whom they added to their aristocracy. For example, the name of the Metelli, one of the largest of later Rome's aristocratic families, appears to originate in the word for a discharged mercenary. One Servius Tullius, who first saw the city as a captive slave boy in a triumphal procession, allegedly went on to become the fifth king of Rome. In contrast to later years, the early Roman nobility was highly accommodating of new members.

As well as those rising to the top from within the state, early Rome also had aristocratic immigrants – for example one Attus Clausus (the ancestor of the accommodating emperor Claudius mentioned above) became disaffected with his native city of Regillum and decamped to Rome with all his household in 504 BC (Livy 2.16.4). As with escaped slaves and bandits on the run, Rome welcomed Clausus with open arms.

Four hundred years later, the descendants of Attus Clausus were known as the Appii Claudii, and any foreign aristocrat was unlikely to get the time of day from them, let alone an invitation to join the senate. True, the aristocracy was prone to regular bursts of xenophobia when it came to outsiders becoming senators. But for most of the senate's existence, individual senators showed a preference for sons-in-law with money and influence whatever their origin. So outsiders could and did join senatorial families and in time their descendants forced their way on to the benches of the senate house. As the emperor Claudius had noted, Volscians, the Aequi, Etruscans and many others eventually became Roman senators – and in time became as wary of outsiders as others had been of their ancestors.

One reason for this exclusivity was that as the Roman state expanded, so did the rewards of being Roman and of holding office in Rome. This is not to say that Rome was corrupt, because 'corruption' implies an alternative system to be corrupted. In ancient Rome nepotism, back-scratching, and the exchange of favours did not corrupt the system – they actually were the system. Without them the administration could not function. The senate was very much an 'old-boy network' and took pride in that fact. If a man had done a senator a favour – such as giving him an interest-free loan – not only would that senator support that man in politics, but he would freely admit the reason.

This worked well when Rome was a small, relatively impoverished city with a warrior aristocracy. When Rome controlled an empire that stretched across the Mediterranean, a 'favour' from a governor or serving consul could be worth millions. Such favours might include the right to collect taxes in a province, a trade monopoly or receipt of a public works contract. Naturally, the person bestowing such a favour expected a cut of those millions, or an equally valuable favour in return. At this point the system started to break down.

It is a truism that power and wealth generally go together, and through the perks of office, those who exercised political power in Rome became extremely wealthy. They had to be, for Rome was still democratic (for a given definition of 'democratic') and competition for votes for public office and its rewards became ferocious. Voters expected to be bribed with gifts, circuses and free dinners. They also rewarded by electing to office those who built civic amenities for them to enjoy, such as fountains, public gardens and temples. The expenses for such amenities came out of a candidate's own pocket. If he was successful in obtaining high office, the candidate could expect to use that office to regain the money he had spent, and a lot more. Those who failed to be elected were often financially ruined.

This had several effects. Firstly politics in Rome – never a gentle occupation – became increasingly cut-throat and the high stakes meant that elections became ever more competitive. Secondly, Roman aristocrats had their hands full competing with one another. They were extremely reluctant to widen the field by allowing outsiders to join the fray. Thirdly, those who were elected to office were those who had the financial resources to woo voters, buy allies and buy off competitors. As time went on and expenses went up, the only people who could afford to pay for all this were those who had held office already and had reaped the huge financial rewards that came with it. Since they had held office, these men did not pay for their own electoral campaigns, but for those of their children. At this point the top jobs in Rome became virtually monopolized by a small group of very wealthy families.

Families that regularly had their members voted to the consulship – the top executive office in Rome – were called the *nobiles*; or as Cicero described them 'those made consuls in their cradles'. Such families were immensely wealthy and hugely influential. Influence was important, for a Roman's *auctoritas* mattered at least as much as his money. *Auctoritas* is a difficult concept to define, but it basically described a man's power to get things done and to prevent others doing things to him. It was a combination of being respected and having a known ability to help others – with the understanding that such help came at a price for the person being helped. *Auctoritas* also included the ability to crush enemies. Political battles often spilled over into the courts, and in such struggles *auctoritas* usually trumped both the law and issues of right and wrong. We shall later (p.78) see the fate of the tribune Varius Hybrida,[1] who was himself accused of the very same charges he failed to press home against an aristocratic Roman and condemned. That was *auctoritas* in action. In rather the same way, when one of the highly aristocratic Metelli was accused of fraud and peculation, none of the jurymen dared look at the accounts presented as evidence because that would show disrespect to Metellus. Naturally Metellus was acquitted.

Throughout Roman history the aristocracy had been powerful. Once Rome had become a Mediterranean-wide empire, the aristocracy reaped a disproportionate share of the rewards and became more powerful still. The *nobiles* controlled access to public office, the administrative functions of the state, the top priestly offices and the courts. But they had always been influential in these areas. The problem came when the *nobiles* began to monopolize land ownership as well. When Rome conquered an enemy, especially in Italy, a commission was sent by the senate to organize how that conquered state would function thereafter. If a city occupied a strategic location, it was highly likely that the original occupants would be displaced and the city occupied by retired Roman legionaries. In such an event, the city became an extension of Rome itself – a *colonus*. More often, Rome made the conquered city an involuntary 'ally' and was content to levy tribute on the original population. This tribute often came in the form of soldiers who then fought alongside the Roman legions in further campaigns. In these cases, Rome also usually took for itself a percentage of the land of the conquered state.

This land was called the *ager publicus*, the 'public field', and as with *colonia*, the intent was to settle discharged legionaries or soldiers from the Italian allies on the land, which they rented from the Roman state at low or nominal rents. In time the sons raised on these smallholdings themselves became eligible for recruitment to the army and the cycle of conquest, settlement and recruitment was repeated. There was a general sentiment that these sturdy sons of peasant stock were the backbone of the army and of Rome's military success.

The young men who stained the Punic Sea with blood …
those who assaulted Pyrrhus,
and struck at great Antiochus,
and fearsome Hannibal –
They were a manly bunch of rustic soldiers
taught to dig the fields with a Sabine hoe,
hauling in the firewood they had cut
at their strict mothers' orders

Horace, Odes 3.4

By the 150s BC Rome was running out of such prime military material. There was a feeling that the peasant farmers were being crowded off the land by the Roman aristocracy. The process was described in detail by the historian Appian who wrote two centuries later. He tells how the Romans created the public land and how it was rented to smallholders, and goes on to say:

They did these things in order to multiply the Italian race, which they considered the most industrious of peoples, so that they might have plenty of allies at home. But the very opposite thing happened; for the rich, getting possession of the greater part of the undistributed lands, and being emboldened by the lapse of time to believe that they would never be dispossessed, absorbing any adjacent strips and their poor neighbours' allotments, partly by purchase under persuasion and partly by force, came to cultivate vast tracts instead of single estates, using slaves as labourers and herdsmen, lest free labourers should be drawn from agriculture into the army.

At the same time the ownership of slaves brought them great gain from the multitude of their progeny, who increased because they were exempt from military service. Thus certain powerful men became extremely rich and the race of slaves multiplied throughout the country, while the Italian people dwindled in numbers and strength, being oppressed by penury, taxes, and military service. If they had any respite from these evils they passed their time in idleness, because the land was held by the rich, who employed slaves instead of freemen as cultivators.

History of Appian 1.1.7, as translated in the Loeb Classical Library
1913

The process of obtaining public land was relatively straightforward for someone with the power and the money to do so. Even though there were laws that allowed only limited parcels of land to be held by a single individual, the nobility simply held their huge estates under the names of proxies, many of whom never even saw the land that they allegedly owned. Those on adjoining lands that the nobility wanted for themselves were literally made an offer they could not refuse. Anyone who did make a stand was forcibly displaced, and since the nobility controlled the courts, there was nowhere to appeal for justice. And to add insult to injury, often the displacement was easily accomplished because the menfolk of a smallholding were away serving in the legions when servants of the nobility came to force the rest of the family from their homes.

Not unexpectedly, this led to a degree of stay-at-home sentiment among the peasantry. This was exacerbated by the fact that at that time Rome was tied up in a drawn-out war in Hispania. Year after year levies went out to the Iberian peninsula, there often to serve several campaigns without release. Mostly the Romans were fighting impoverished tribesmen who were very good at fighting back, so for the recruits the chance of an untimely death was high while the chance of returning from the wars with any worthwhile booty was low.

Not just Romans but their Italian allies suffered the injustice of being displaced from their land while they were fighting in wars that brought profit and glory only to the very aristocrats who took their farms while they were gone. In fact the Italians suffered worse than the Romans because a Roman citizen was also a voter, and the aristocracy coveted the votes of citizens. So if a substantial bloc of voters in a particular area felt aggrieved, they could take their case to Rome and get a sympathetic hearing in exchange for their votes in the next election.

Italians had no such protection. They could and did complain loudly. However, there were no votes to be obtained from Italians, so no aristocrat had anything to gain by taking their case. On the other hand, the aristocrat the Italians were complaining about would certainly take offence with anyone who listened to such complaints. Therefore anyone who took up the cause of Italians unfairly dispossessed of their lands would be making a powerful enemy of the aristocratic dispossessor and getting nothing in return. So the Italians had few defenders in Rome, and by the middle of the second century the Italian peninsula was steaming with resentment.

The dispossessed had two choices. They could go to the towns and try to make a living there, or they could re-enrol in the legions for year after year, renting the land that would nominally give them the property qualification that was at this time required of a Roman soldier. (Being desperate for manpower, the army seldom enquired too searchingly into these qualifications.)

Another problem was that while the estates of the rich were extensive, cash crops such as wine, figs and olives provided higher revenues than the wheat and barley produced by the average smallholder. Therefore the amount of land under grain cultivation fell, so that 'the nourishing grain runs out and there is no bread for the common people' as the contemporary poet Lucilius put it.[2]

Declining military manpower, an increasingly precarious food supply, massive resentment among the common people and ever-more mutinous allies – the self-absorbed greed of the Roman nobility had certainly managed to create an abundance of problems. Even some members of the Roman nobility noticed it.

The first to contemplate a political solution to the problem was one Gaius Laelius, a friend of Scipio Aemilianus, the soldier famous for destroying Carthage and winning the intractable Numantine War in Iberia. Scipio Aemilianus himself made a few half-hearted attempts to approach the matter, but quickly withdrew after he discovered that showing sympathy for land reform made it easy for enemies such as his rival Appius Claudius to turn the senate against him. Laelius was hardly more effective. In the 140s he introduced to the senate an agrarian bill that addressed some of the worst abuses of the aristocracy, but he was apparently unprepared for the uproar that resulted. He hastily backed down.

Gaius Laelius, a comrade of Scipio made an attempt to rectify this evil, but those with influence resisted the proposals. Fearing the consequences which might follow, he abandoned the issue, and for so doing he was nicknamed Sapiens ('the wise').

Plutarch, *Life of Tiberius Gracchus* 8

However, for all that the senate studiously ignored it, the issue did not go away. The next to raise the matter of land reform as a political issue was a young man from the very highest level of Roman society. This was a grandson of the great Scipio Africanus, the conqueror of Hannibal; the son of the prominent politician and general Sempronius Longus. His name was Tiberius Gracchus, and he had an axe to grind.

Like many young aristocrats, Tiberius had gone to fight in the Iberian wars. His father, Sempronius, had done this too, and won not only great distinction among the Romans, but even the admiration of the Spaniards. Given that most Roman generals in Iberia had a penchant for wholesale plunder, massacre and treachery, all Sempronius had to do to gain a reputation for fair dealing with the enemy was to show restraint, and actually keep his word once he had given it.

This was fortunate for Rome a generation later, because the army with which Tiberius was a junior officer was trapped by the Celtiberians in an untenable position. Twenty thousand Roman soldiers faced death by massacre or starvation, so not unexpectedly the Roman general attempted to negotiate. The Celtiberians would only deal with Tiberius, because they trusted his father's reputation. Though still only a young man, Tiberius managed to negotiate not only the safe withdrawal of the endangered army but an equitable peace treaty with the Celtiberians.

Tiberius may have felt proud of his achievement. If so he would have been totally unprepared for the storm of execration that greeted his return to Rome. No matter how fair the treaty he had negotiated, the fact that he had negotiated it from a position of weakness made the agreement totally unacceptable to the senate. Instead of being praised for saving an army of twenty thousand men, Tiberius was in danger of being prosecuted for being one of the officers who had got that army into danger in the first place. Only the intervention of Scipio Aemilianus saved Tiberius from the fate of his commanding officer, who was delivered in chains to the Celtiberians. The treaty to which Tiberius had pledged his word and his honour was unequivocally repudiated. Having got its army back safely, the senate saw no reason not to continue its war against the people who had spared it. For Tiberius the shock, humiliation and dishonour were intense, and being as proud and stubborn as only a Roman aristocrat could be, he did not take it lying down.

While the senate might sneer at Tiberius for being a turncoat Celtiberian sympathizer, the relatives of the twenty thousand common soldiers had a different perspective – and many of those relatives were voters. Therefore, when Tiberius decided to stand for political office, the choice of which office was obvious. He would become Tribune of the Plebs, Rome's advocate for the common man.

A Tribune of the Plebs had a great deal of power if he cared to use it. The office had been forced on the senate by the people of Rome as protection against abuse by the aristocracy. A tribune could present proposals to legislative assemblies. He could veto motions of the senate. In extreme situations he could even arrest the consuls. However, the powers of a tribune did not extend beyond the boundaries of the city of Rome itself. Therefore tribunes had been of little value to Romans dispossessed of their land in the countryside, and of no use whatsoever to Italians in the same position. This was particularly so because, as with almost all other institutions of the Roman state, the tribunate had been captured by the nobility. Tribunes of the second century were noblemen who used their positions mainly to participate in the political struggles of the aristocracy without much regard for the purposes for which the office had originally been created. Tiberius planned to change all that.

There was a faction in the senate quietly pressing for land reform. This faction was led by two brothers of the Mucius Scaevola family and their relative Licinius Crassus Mucianus – all three persons of no little influence. Very well, Tiberius would take up their cause and force the rich to return the lands they had unfairly taken. By doing this, Tiberius would further endear himself to the common voter, correct a major problem that was poisoning economic and political life in the Italian peninsula and simultaneously deliver a vigorous kick to the highly deserving derrières of the nobility in the senate. Overall, the plan appeared to have no downside. Tiberius was an eloquent speaker, and he set about persuading the people to vote for his legislation. The biographer Plutarch quotes from a speech attributed to Tiberius Gracchus, which gives some of the flavour of his oratory.

> The wild beasts of Italy have each a cave or a lair of their own. But the men who fight and die for Italy have no part of it but the sunlight and air. With their wives and children they wander from place to place with neither hearth nor home.
>
> So the lips of their generals lie when before battle they exhort the soldiers to defend their family tombs and shrines from the enemy, because not a man of their listeners has an hereditary altar, no, not one of all these many Romans has an ancestral tomb. Instead they fight and die to support others in wealth and luxury. Yet they are called masters of the world, these men who have not a single lump of earth to call their own.
>
> Plutarch, *Life of Tiberius Gracchus* 9

With eloquence, justice and the people on his side there seemed no way that Tiberius could not get his way. But appearances were deceptive. The Roman nobility had many faults, but weakness and cowardice were not among them. In fact a believer in eugenics might point out that by 133 BC (the year Tiberius became tribune) the Roman aristocracy had been breeding for stubbornness, ruthlessness and decisiveness for about five hundred years, and now were very stubborn, ruthless and decisive. Furthermore its members regarded the 'public lands' as their private property. Some had been given them as dowries, others were using these lands as security for loans. Many had received the lands as inheritance from fathers whose tombs were now on the property. They would not surrender easily.

The first step of the aristocrats was to suborn one of Tiberius' fellow tribunes, a man called Marcus Octavius. This was not too hard, as Octavius was himself a noble who held a substantial tract of what should have been public land. When Tiberius proposed his agrarian law, Marcus Octavius exercised his tribune's right to veto legislation, and forbade its passing. Under the Roman constitution, a veto always took precedence over an affirmative action so Tiberius' legislation was killed on the spot. However, Tiberius was also a Roman noble, and as proud and stubborn as the rest. He immediately withdrew his planned law, and proposed another even more severe by which those who had occupied public land were to be dispossessed in turn, immediately and without compensation. By way of encouraging acceptance of his law, Tiberius raised the stakes yet higher. He used his veto against any and all public functions of the Roman state, so that salaries could not be paid and law courts could not function – in short the governance of Rome was brought to a standstill until the senate permitted a public vote on his proposal.

When matters did come to a vote, the voting urns that served as ballot boxes in ancient Rome mysteriously vanished, along with the votes within them. And Octavius vetoed a further vote. Tiberius still would not back down, but instead took the legally dubious step of ordering a different vote – to have Octavius recalled from office. With Octavius removed, the agrarian legislation was passed, but the manner of its passing left a sour taste in the mouths of many, who felt that the manner of Octavius' removal had weakened and debased the tribunate. The enemies of Tiberius waited eagerly for his time in office to be over, for a tribune was sacrosanct – safe from prosecution and defended by the plebs against physical violence. As a private citizen Tiberius was highly vulnerable. When it became apparent that the turbulent tribune planned to stand for re-election the following year the frustration of the nobility boiled over. When Tiberius was holding a public meeting his enemies in the senate took action – decisively and ruthlessly.

The senators wrapped their togas about their left arms, and shoved aside those in their way. No-one opposed men of such authority but instead they fell over each other in their attempts to get away. The servants of the senators brought clubs and staffs from their homes, but the senators had already seized upon the legs of benches broken by the fleeing crowd. With these they attacked those trying to shield Tiberius, slaughtering some and routing the rest. Tiberius turned to run, but his clothing was held, so he shed his toga and fled in his tunic, only to stumble and fall over some bodies on the ground in front of him. As he struggled to his feet he took the first blow …

Plutarch, *Life of Tiberius* 19

Tiberius was beaten to death on the spot along with some three hundred of his supporters. The leader of the senatorial lynch mob was Tiberius' cousin, Scipio Nasica, Pontifex Maximus and chief priest of the Roman state (and incidentally a large landholder of public land). He was foremost among those who thereafter led a purge against the supporters of Tiberius.

Tiberius was dead and his supporters persecuted, but his cause lived on. The senatorial supporters of Scipio Nasica had gone too far. Public revulsion at the brutal slaying threatened to tear Rome apart, and cooler heads among the aristocracy intervened. The sides were too polarized for anyone to admit talking to their opponents, but all the signs are that a deal was reached. Tiberius' law was law, and it would stand, not least because it was clear to most that land redistribution was needed. Many of those formerly in opposition had been opposed to Tiberius and his methods rather than what he was trying to achieve. Now (as the later Roman writer Valerius Maximus put it) both the author of the problem and the problem itself were resolved by the death of Tiberius and the acceptance of his laws.

In exchange for accepting their leader's lynching, Tiberius' supporters also demanded a further sacrifice from their opponents – and got it. Although traditionally the Pontifex Maximus did not leave Rome, Scipio Nasica the lyncher-in-chief was found duties to perform in Asia Minor, and once there Scipio was firmly instructed not to come back. Though no one called it such, this was exile. Scipio died shortly afterwards in the Anatolian city of Pergamon (foul play was suspected).

In Italy, the land redistribution went ahead. As might be expected of a proposal that required legislative support from the voters, Tiberius' land legislation had been aimed primarily at Roman citizens. As popular enthusiasm for land redistribution gathered pace, opportunist Roman politicians threw their support behind the measure but always with an eye to how many votes were in it for themselves. Not unexpectedly under these circumstances, those on the short end of the stick were the disenfranchised Italian allies of Rome who were now worse off than before. When conquered by Rome in decades or even centuries past many Italians who had their lands converted into *ager publicus* had simply continued to occupy those lands as tenants. Now all this was thrown into confusion.

Wherever a new field adjoining an old one had been bought, or divided among the allies, the whole district had to be carefully inquired into, on account of the measurement of this one field, to discover how it had been sold and how divided. Not all owners had preserved their contracts, or their allotment titles, and even those that were found were often ambiguous. When the land was resurveyed, some owners were obliged to give up their fruit-trees and farm-buildings in exchange for naked ground. Others were transferred from cultivated to uncultivated lands, or to swamps, or pools. ... The Italian allies complained of these disturbances, and especially of the lawsuits hastily brought against them. ...the consul Tuditanus was appointed to give judgement in these cases. But when he took up the work he saw the difficulties of it, and marched against the Illyrians as a pretext for not acting as judge, and nobody brought cases for trial.

Appian, *Civil Wars* 1.18 as translated
in the Loeb Classical Library, 1913

The deadlock played into the hands of the nobility who either used one pretext or the other to avoid transferring title of the public lands that they occupied, or bluntly refused to give it up. Others ceded land to Roman citizens, but compensated themselves with illegal land grabs from Italians. Those awarded title to disputed land had to go to court to obtain possession, but nobody was hearing such cases.

Eventually a Gracchan sympathizer called Fulvius Flaccus proposed a solution. Most of those protesting about the land redistribution were the Italian allies; unsurprising since both those allocating the land and the courts (when they made a decision at all) favoured Roman citizens. The solution was straightforward. Make the Italian allies Roman citizens. After all, entire Italian communities had been made citizens in the past, and Rome had benefited mightily thereby. Why not do it again?

This would have a double effect on land disputes. Firstly, with the prospect of Roman citizenship offered as compensation, many Italian communities would be content with the inferior land deals they were currently being offered. Secondly, when a land dispute came before a Roman magistrate, both plaintiffs and defendants would be Roman citizens, and the magistrate – who was also a politician seeking re-election – would make a fairer decision if he alienated one set of voters in the course of appeasing another. At present the magistrate adjudicating a land dispute could appease the Romans and let the Italians go hang, and he generally did just that. Those Italians who wished to remain independent of the Roman body politic, proposed Flaccus, should have the right of appeal against 'tyrannical' decisions by Roman magistrates.

Many Italians had already taken the shortest route to the citizenship possible. Once dispossessed from their land they had moved to Rome, and after dwelling in the city for a number of years they applied to the censors for permission to be considered for Roman citizenship. While waiting, they made a point of turning up at political assemblies and heckling speakers whom they considered unsympathetic to their cause. So many took this step that Junius Pennus, the tribune for 126/5, passed a law forbidding non-Romans access to the city, claiming that it was draining Italian municipalities of their populations.

The proposal of Flaccus that the citizenship be dramatically widened to include the Italian allies presented the ancient world with a radical new idea – that a man could be a citizen of two states at once. Previously being made into Romans – whether voluntarily by individuals, or compulsorily under the *cives sine suffragio* system – had meant totally abandoning one's former national identity. The idea that one might be a solid burgher of – for example – Fidenae and simultaneously be a Roman voter required a mental adjustment that neither Romans nor Italians were prepared for. The Roman people were confused by Flaccus' proposal or indifferent to it, and the idea failed to gain much traction. The senate, on the other hand, understood the proposal and were downright hostile. When Flaccus appeared in the senate house to explain his proposals he received earnest imprecations from the senators to drop the plan, and veiled threats about what would happen if he did not. Like Laelius before him, Flaccus decided that the personal price of pushing reform was too high. He abandoned his proposal and went to take out his frustrations against the Gauls in a military campaign. However, the idea that Flaccus had dropped rippled through Italian minds, and over the decades that ripple was to grow, and grow into a veritable tsunami that almost swept away Rome itself.

It is not as if Rome was not warned. As soon as it was clear that the Flaccan proposal had been dropped, Rome was given a taste of what was to come a generation later. The Italians of the city of Fregellae rose in rebellion. On the left bank of the River Liris in Latium, situated amid rich farmland, Fregellae was no minor city but one of the largest and most flourishing cities in the region. That such a city was prepared to risk everything in a rebellion should have set off warning bells in the minds of Roman politicians that the citizenship was becoming a major issue.

This warning should have been all the more urgent because until then Fregellae had been no nest of malcontents, but instead one of Rome's most loyal allies. When Hannibal had marched on the region in 212 BC, the people of Fregellae sent warning post-haste to Rome, and then destroyed the bridges across the river Liris by which Hannibal would get there – even though this meant that the disgruntled Hannibal would instead devastate the lands of Fregellae (which he did indeed devastate comprehensively). Despite this devastation, in 209 BC when a dozen Roman colonies rebelled against Rome's constant demands for manpower to continue fighting Hannibal, Fregellae led the delegates who went to Rome to pledge their loyalty.

The reaction of the Roman senate to Fregellae's defection was predictable, and did not involve much soul-searching. Instead of pondering about how they had managed to alienate even this most faithful of allies, the Romans reacted in the way they knew best – decisively and ruthlessly. The praetor Lucius Opimus took an army and flattened Fregellae so comprehensively that today archaeologists cannot say for certain where the city once stood. To make sure that Fregellae never rose again, the Romans founded the rival city of Fabrateria nearby, which then took over the lands and trade that had once sustained Fregellae. The grim example of Fregellae may have deterred other Italian cities contemplating rebellion from putting the idea into practice, but it did not remove the reasons why rebellion was contemplated in the first place. However, the use of extreme force to suppress dissent bought the senate some time to sort out the tangle of land rights and citizenship that bedevilled the state. It did not use that time wisely.

For a start, dealing with both land reform and citizenship became vastly more complex because, as so often happened in the Roman Republic, personalities interfered with policies. The cause of land reform and Roman citizenship was taken up by someone who was in many ways the worst man for the job – Gaius Gracchus, the brother of the late, lynched Tiberius. Not that Gaius was lacking honesty, energy and competence. He had all three, and was intelligent and politically astute as well. But he was the brother of Tiberius Gracchus. This meant that Gaius was considered an enemy of the group in the senate who had connived at his brother's death. This group was in fact partly defined by opposition to anything Gracchan, and its members called themselves the optimates (the best men). Not only did they consider Gaius Gracchus as being automatically their enemy, but they were right to do so. Any Roman noble who overlooked the murder of a brother would have been thought a spineless wimp and politically negligible in any case.

In fact Gaius, as he had to, pursued a dual agenda of harassing the optimates and pushing for further land reform and citizenship for the Italian allies. The optimates pushed right back, resisting every step of the way, thus making land reform and citizenship partisan issues just when a consensus was essential. Had young Gaius Gracchus been killed by a Sardinian rebel while he was doing his military service on the island, matters of land reform and citizenship would not have been dropped. Instead they would have found a different, less divisive champion; and in fact one was available. This was none other than Fulvius Flaccus. It will be remembered that Flaccus had dropped the issue of citizenship and gone off to campaign in Gaul. Well, he had campaigned so successfully that he was largely responsible for setting the province of Gallia Transalpina on a secure basis (a job ably completed by his successor Quintus Fabius Maximus). Now with the prestige of a triumph over the Ligurian tribe to add to his authority, and with his political potency supplemented by the wealth of his booty, Flaccus was ready once again to take up the cause of enfranchising the Italian allies. Except Gaius Gracchus had beaten him to it.

This was unfortunate, as Flaccus had never alienated the optimates in the senate. Gaius had accomplished that simply by being Tiberius' brother, and thereafter he happily burned any bridges that led to a reconciliation. As everyone expected, despite the strong resistance of the optimates – who accused him of anything they thought might stick, including fomenting the rebellion at Fregellae – Gaius Gracchus became Tribune of the Plebs in his turn. As tribune Gaius persecuted those behind his brother's killing and drove into exile Popillius, an ex-consul who had led the purge of Tiberius' followers. Gaius also expanded his brother's land reform legislation and cracked down on those who had evaded its provisions. It is uncertain whether the pain this caused the nobility was incidental or the reason for the new legislation, but it certainly did not endear Gaius to the senate.

Rather than compete with Gaius for leadership of his faction, Flaccus threw his support behind the young tribune and the two became close political allies. So close in fact that the year 122 BC saw the unusual sight of an ex-consul sitting on the tribune's bench. Flaccus had chosen to be elected to the post along with Gaius Gracchus.

It is uncertain to what extent Flaccus demanded that Gaius Gracchus give greater weight to the cause of citizenship for the Italian allies as the price for his support, and to what extent Gaius – already a supporter of the idea – promoted the measure on his own account. In any case, in 123 Gaius Gracchus pressed the case for enfranchising the Italians with more urgency. Enfranchising the allies would have bestowed one huge advantage on Gaius – if he got the Italians the vote, they would be forever grateful. That gratitude would translate into votes, so not only Gaius Gracchus but his family and descendants would be paramount in Italian politics for the foreseeable future. This prospect terrified the optimates, and any chance of consensus on the citizenship issue became utterly impossible.

Nevertheless, Gaius Gracchus felt he did not need consensus to get his way. He had already pushed through a huge mass of legislation the previous year, which covered everything from building roads across Italy, founding large numbers of colonies in Italy and abroad (including controversially, one on the former site of Carthage), and laws restricting the role of the senate in the law courts and tax collection. Much of this also the optimates had resented and resisted, but ineffectually. Therefore as January brought in the year 122 Gracchus made his first move toward enfranchising the allies. This was not to be a sweeping measure such as Flaccus had unsuccessfully proposed almost four years previously, but a measured pace in the right direction.

There already existed a halfway house towards the Roman citizenship known as the Latin Right. This right was originally given to the peoples of Latium to compensate for the dissolution of the Latin League in 338 BC. It allowed Latins the same mutual privileges as they had enjoyed under the league – that is *commercium*, *connubium* and the *ius migrationis*. This meant that anyone with Latin rights could make a legal contract with someone else possessing such rights, could legally marry such a person, and could move to another Latin city and obtain citizenship thereof. The Latin Right had been extended well beyond Latium as the Roman empire expanded.

One reason why the Latin Right was so desirable was because Rome sponsored it and therefore the privileges of the Latin Right were protected by Roman law. Consequently someone with the Latin Right who held a land contract could insist that the Roman courts enforce that contract. It has been seen that the Roman courts were often lax in their duty, but even this was better than nothing. Other Italians had not even that much recourse.

So now Gaius Gracchus proposed that the present holders of the Latin Right become Romans, and the other Italian allies should get the Latin Right. From there, with the precedent established, a process would exist by which conquered people could first become involuntary allies, then Latins and finally Roman citizens. This, as with much of Gaius Gracchus' other legislation, was reasonable, far-sighted and addressed one of the fundamental problems underlying the structure of the Roman Republic. Also, as with much of Gaius Gracchus' other legislation, the optimates were determined that it should not pass, if for no other reason than it was proposed by Gaius Gracchus and would greatly benefit Gaius Gracchus. So when the measure was brought to the vote, the tribune Livius Drusus vetoed it. It was harder for Gaius Gracchus to get rid of Livius Drusus than it was for Tiberius Gracchus to get rid of his obdurate fellow tribune Octavius. For a start the Roman people remained dubious of the legality of voting a tribune out of office and secondly, it turned out that the Roman people didn't want to vote Livius Drusus out.

The senate was trying a new tactic. They would use Drusus to outflank Gaius Gracchus on the flank he least expected to have to defend. Drusus simply out-demagogued the populist Gaius. If Gaius proposed to found three colonies of Roman citizens, Drusus proposed twelve. If Gaius proposed easing the rents on public land, Drusus announced the rents should be abolished altogether. Not unexpectedly the Roman voters loved this bidding war for their favour and were not at all prepared to remove any of the participants from the political stage. So Gaius Gracchus had to put up with Livius Drusus, and while Livius Drusus was prepared to go further than Gracchus in almost any direction, he drew the line at extending the citizenship. This he vetoed, and there was nothing Gaius Gracchus could do about it.

The franchise proposal was seen by the senate as the weakest point of Gaius Gracchus' platform. The Roman voter could not see how the proposal could be of direct benefit, and like the senate, the common Roman was jealous of his privileges. Even Fannius, a former ally whom Gaius had helped to the consulship now turned on his sponsor in a speech to the Roman people.

> So you will give citizenship to the Latins? And afterwards do you imagine that there will be space to do as you are now doing and listen to a public meeting? Or find room at the games or public festivals? Why don't you stop and think? If you did you'd see that they will crowd you out of everything.
>
> Fannius, via Cicero and Iulus Victor 6.4

When the crucial vote came, Fannius as consul ordered all non-voters out of the city. This weakened Gaius Gracchus, as though non-voters, the allies were powerful and effective hecklers. Seduced by the promises of Livius Drusus and worried by the insinuations of Fannius, the voters decided they did not need more Romans than they already had. The franchise motion was quashed.

Gaius Gracchus continued in office, but his wings had been clipped. The year 121 was approaching, when Gaius' tribunate would expire. As an ominous portent the grim Opimius, destroyer of Fregellae and avowed enemy of all things Gracchan, was voted consul for the coming year. As a further proof of weakening support for his cause, Gaius himself was not re-elected tribune. Actually, his biographer Plutarch says he was elected 'but his colleagues cheated and produced fraudulent returns'.[3] Possibly with the hindsight that comes from writing centuries after subsequent events, Plutarch says Gaius Gracchus turned on those mocking him and retorted 'theirs was sardonic laughter [i.e. the laughter of the doomed] for they could not see the coming great darkness that was the consequence of their measures'.

Once Gaius was out of office, his enemies circled, ever agitating, ever waiting for a chance to strike. Opimius, to no one's surprise, immediately called a series of legislative assemblies aimed at repealing the laws passed by Gaius while he was in office. (The populist measures passed by Drusus appear to have been generally ignored and were quietly allowed to lapse.) Gaius Gracchus and his partisans naturally opposed this, and tensions in Rome mounted as violence and bloodshed between the factions intensified. Eventually the senate turned to the consul Opimius and urged him to 'see to it that the state took no harm'. Opimius took this announcement as tantamount to a declaration of martial law, with himself as judge, jury and executioner under that law.

The Gracchan faction was armed and ready to defend itself against mob violence, but not against the organized force that Opimius brought to bear. He rejected peace overtures, even when Flaccus sent his own son as an envoy. Cretan archers and militia easily overcame the resistance of the Gracchan partisans who were offered immunity if they abandoned their leader. For Gracchus himself a reward was offered equal to the weight of his head in gold. Those claiming the reward had only to offer the head – the remainder of the body was not required. Once Gracchus was dead, Opimius reneged on his offer of immunity, and led a purge that made the witch-hunt of Tiberius' supporters look tame. Some three thousand Gracchan supporters were arbitrarily sentenced to death in kangaroo courts – in such cases considered worth the semblance of judicial process. As he had done with Fregellae, Opimius was thorough and merciless. The property of the slain was confiscated by the public treasury, and wives were forbidden to go into mourning. Then, to add insult to injury, Opimius used the confiscated funds to erect a temple of Concord in the forum by way of a victory monument.

It was a comprehensive victory. The Gracchus brothers were dead, and the cause of Italian enfranchisement so poisoned that no one would touch it for thirty years. Yet as Gaius Gracchus had prophesied, the victory of his enemies would bring only darkness. The festering cause of Italian citizenship would spread into the equally poisonous rivalry between the two greatest Romans of the next generation. Not only would this bring down a cataclysm upon Italy, but it would also wipe out the sons of those very senators who now rejoiced in their temporary triumph.

Chapter 2

The Rivals

The deaths of the Gracchus brothers put the matter of enfranchising the allies on hold. This did not mean that the issue went away – it simply meant that nobody dared to deal with it. Certainly the Italian allies felt no more warmly towards Rome. However, the deaths of their champions meant that there was no one to take up their cause within Rome itself, and the example of Fregellae demonstrated that unilateral action had disastrous consequences. Meanwhile Roman arrogance continued to infuriate the Italians. Gaius Gracchus had given some examples of this before he died, and after his death this conduct continued.

The consul recently came to [the town of] Teanum Sidicinum. His wife wished to bathe in the men's baths. Marcus Marius, the quaestor [roughly 'mayor'] of Sidicinum, was instructed to send away the bathers from the baths. The wife informed her husband that the baths were not given up to her soon enough and that they were not clean enough. Therefore a stake was planted in the forum and Marcus Marius, the most illustrious man of his city, was led to it. His clothing was stripped off, he was whipped with rods. The people of Cales, when they heard of this, passed a decree that no one should think of using the public baths when a Roman magistrate was in town...

I will give you a single example of the lawlessness of our young men, and of their entire lack of self-control. Within the last few years a young man who had not yet held office as a Roman magistrate was sent as an envoy from Asia. He was carried in a litter. A herdsman, one of the peasants of Venusia, met him, and not knowing whom they were bearing, jokingly asked the litter-bearers if they were carrying a corpse. Upon hearing this, the young man ordered that the litter be set down and that the peasant be beaten to death.

Orf 2 via Gell NA 10.3

With the complacency that followed their 'victory', the Roman aristocracy saw no need to mend their ways. The Italian allies were Roman subjects, and they would simply have to do as they were told. Yet at the same time, the Romans insisted that the Italian allies supply their army with troops trained and armoured to the standard of Roman legionaries. The incompatibility of these two polices – treating the Italians as a conquered people, and simultaneously insisting that they have large numbers of highly competent soldiery ready for action – never appears to have struck the senate as dangerous enough to worry about.

Partly this was because the Italians themselves were not a homogeneous group that might easily form a joint cause against Rome. As will be seen, the Italians were as diverse as the peoples of modern Europe are today. The Greek-speaking peoples of the south had very little in common with the Gauls in the north, and neither of these two nations could understand the Samnites of the central interior. Rome's famed technique of 'divide and conquer' continued to hold down Italy even after most of that peninsula had in fact been conquered. Individual Italians who reached a certain status within a community might individually aspire to the citizenship that Rome denied to their fellow burghers, and individual communities competed with one another for the Latin Right, or simply for Roman patrons among the aristocracy. Among the Italians mutual incomprehension of each other's language and culture, together with rivalry for Roman favour prevented them from working together, and the Romans smugly assumed it would always be so.

Meanwhile, lacking any sort of check, the Roman aristocracy became ever more oligarchic, self-interested and corrupt. This was highlighted by the appalling mismanagement of the Jugurthine war that broke out in Africa a decade after Gaius Gracchus was killed. Jugurtha was the adopted son of king Micipsa of Numidia. On Micipsa's death Jugurtha became king by assassinating one of Micipsa's natural sons. The surviving son appealed to Rome, which sent a commission to divide the kingdom between him and Jugurtha. The resultant settlement so favoured Jugurtha that it seems certain that the commission's members were bribed. In 113 BC Jugurtha declared war on his rival, and drove him into the city of Cirta. A delegation came from Rome to tell Jugurtha to desist, but all that happened was that the delegates went home wealthy men and the siege of Cirta continued. When Jugurtha took Cirta, he killed his rival, and also a number of Italians who were in the city at the time.

With the Italians complaining furiously, Rome was forced to declare war. Jugurtha immediately and enthusiastically surrendered, and in return was allowed without punishment to basically keep all he had gained. Again it seems certain that the consul who arranged the peace settlement was massively bribed. The peace treaty was so blatantly slanted in Jugurtha's favour that it caused an uproar in Rome, and the miscreant king was summoned to explain to a court of enquiry how he had managed to obtain such favourable terms. However, two tribunes – evidently also bribed – used their veto to prevent Jugurtha from testifying, and consequently the court of enquiry failed to unearth a single fact. For Jugurtha the trip to Rome was not a total waste, because while he was there he arranged for the assassination of a cousin who had fled to the Romans for asylum. Ordered out of the city by indignant Romans, Jugurtha is said to have looked back as he departed, and remarked 'That entire city is for sale. It's doomed if it finds a buyer.'[1]

Next up for sale was the propraetor Aulus Postumius Albinus. Tired of Jugurtha's broken promises and flagrant contempt, Rome sent a new army to Numidia to bring the renegade king to heel. Not unexpectedly, given that it was commanded by a Roman aristocrat, the army made a bee-line for the city of Suthul, which was alleged to hold Jugurtha's very substantial treasury. The historian Sallust takes up the tale of what happened next.

Jugurtha well knew that the commander was both arrogant and incompetent. So he further swelled the man's head by sending envoys who begged for peace while he himself moved his army away through the woods and footpaths. Finally, by holding out hope of an agreement, he induced Aulus to leave [the siege of] Suthul and follow him as he pretended to withdraw into a remote region... Meanwhile the king's most cunning emissaries worked day and night on the Roman army. Centurions and cavalry commanders were bribed either to desert or to abandon their posts when told to do so.

Once he had everything set the way he wanted it, Jugurtha suddenly surrounded the Roman camp in the dead of night... Then from the number of those who had been bribed, (as I have mentioned above), one cohort of Ligurians with two squadrons of Thracians and a number of individual soldiers went over to the king, while the chief centurion of the Third Legion allowed the enemy to enter the part of the fortifications which he had been appointed to guard. All the Numidians burst in ...

Sallust, *Jugurthine War* 38ff

Albinus was forced to surrender. He agreed that he and his army would quit Africa within ten days, and Jugurtha forced the Romans to pass under the yoke – a ritual by which an ancient army accepted that it had been totally defeated and survived only at the enemy's sufferance. Having an entire Roman army captured and humiliated certainly caught the attention of a people who had come to look on victory as their birthright. Naturally enough, given its previous form, the senate promptly reneged on the terms of the treaty made by Albinus, and ordered that his army should remain in Africa. However, the men of this army were utterly demoralized, and incapable of carrying out any further military operations. The common people of Rome were furious.

The tribune Mamilius Limetanus proposed a law that a commission should be set up to investigate and punish those whose greed and complacency had let matters get this far. Not unexpectedly, the nobility did everything it could to prevent this commission from starting work, but the Roman populace was relentless. 'They passed the bill with incredible keenness and enthusiasm; not from patriotic fervour, but because it would cause trouble for the nobility whom they hated,' reports Sallust.[2] 'The investigation was conducted with harshness and violence, on hearsay evidence and at the whim of the mob.' The people took particular pleasure in bringing charges against L. Opimius. The man who had flattened Fregellae and ordered the killing of thousands of Gracchan supporters was accused of enriching himself as one of the commissioners who had originally divided Numidia between Jugurtha and the surviving son of Micipsa. The court found him guilty – as he almost certainly was – and Opimius was forced from Rome, later to die as a disgraced exile in Greece.

Thereafter, the senate was compelled to take drastic steps to deal with the Numidian situation. Previous generals had been chosen on their ability to politik their way to a position of command from which they hoped to enrich themselves. Now the senate had to select a general for his ability to actually command armies, a man who was more interested in winning battles than booty. At least, the senators consoled themselves, they were able to find such a man among their own ranks – one Quintus Caecilius Metellus. Elected consul in 109 BC, Metellus went off to the war. Whether he liked it or not, he had to take with him as his second-in-command a man called Caius Marius.

As one of the main protagonists of the catastrophe that struck the Roman Republic in the years 91–81 BC, Caius Marius deserves our close attention. He was a man of great energy and ambition, as was demonstrated by the fact that he had forced himself into the largely closed ranks of Rome's governing class. Marius was also a politician to the core, and the sort of politician who gives the breed a bad name. He was unscrupulous and immoral, and did not care what persons or principles he sacrificed so long as the sacrifice helped his rise to the top. Ordinarily Marius would have been indistinguishable from the dozens of other minor politicians infesting Rome at the time, but Marius also had intelligence, exceptional ability as an organizer and an opportunistic ability to pick his moment. (As it transpired, these same factors later made him a very good general.)

Despite the claim of his biographer Plutarch that Marius' father was a common labourer, it is much more probable that Marius was from the *domi nobiles* – the lesser aristocracy of the Italian cities. As such, though an outsider among the oligarchs who governed Rome, Marius had contacts with the oligarchs as these men valued the *domi nobiles* as clients of their patronage. Thus we first meet Marius as a junior but valued member of the retinue of Scipio Aemilianus when he went to war to avenge the defeat by the Numidians which so disgraced Tiberius Gracchus. (Another under Scipio's command in that war, leading a unit of Numidian cavalry, was the young Jugurtha. This suggests that Scipio picked his men for ability rather than scruples.)

After making his name for himself in Iberia, Marius returned to Rome. Here he won the backing of the Metellus clan when he made a bid for the tribunate. However, once elected tribune Marius cheerfully turned against everything the aristocratic Metelli stood for, and became unabashedly demagogic. Among other measures, he proposed a law that prevented the aristocracy from interfering in electoral ballots. These measures were good for Roman democracy, but it seems improbable that Marius chose to force them through on that basis. Rather, he had decided that the votes of the common people were of more value to him than the support of the Metelli who had got him his office. When he was summoned before the senate to explain himself, Marius stood his ground. When the consul called on Metellus as Marius' patron to talk sense into his protégé, Marius signalled the end of that particular relationship by having Metellus arrested for interfering with a tribune in the course of his duties. Thereafter Marius' law went through, but he had made an enemy of the Metelli, who rather justifiably felt that Marius had both stabbed them in the back and demeaned the family name in front of their colleagues.

Metellan enmity made further political progress difficult. After completing his year as tribune, Marius tried to get elected as aedile, and failed. It appeared that abandoning the favour of the Metelli in exchange for the favour of the common voters had been a misjudgement, but Marius persevered. He eventually gained the office of praetor, a rank second only to the consul, though he had to bribe his way to winning the election, and the Metelli made sure he was prosecuted for it. The trial went badly for Marius, so it came as a surprise when the jury failed to condemn him. Almost certainly a deal was made with someone behind the scenes, though we know not with whom. There were many people for whom it was useful to have a serving praetor owing a substantial favour.

As praetor Marius served capably but without great distinction in Spain, and on his return he cast about for allies in Rome. He took as a wife a woman called Julia of the up-and-coming family of the Julii Caesares,[3] and awaited his next opportunity. The disastrous war in Africa was tailor-made for Marius to promote himself further. We do not know what odd combination of pledges given and called in resulted in Marius being selected as the foremost of Metellus' subordinates, but it is unlikely that Marius was the man that Metellus himself would have chosen. But chosen he was, and the way the system worked meant that Metellus himself had to nominate that choice to the senate, so he must have reconciled himself – however reluctantly – with his recalcitrant ex-client.

It was not long before Metellus regretted his choice. It was clear almost from the start that Marius had joined the African army with the long-term aim of taking control of it for himself. Since the army already had a general in command, and finally a rather good one too, Marius had first to set about undermining his boss. His first step was one that Metellus could not really complain about, since Marius worked at winning the loyalty of the men. 'It is a most agreeable spectacle for a Roman soldier to see a general eating common bread in public, sleeping on a simple pallet, or helping with the construction of some trench or palisade' remarks Marius' biographer Plutarch,[4] and Marius did all this and more.

Metellus had chosen to beat Jugurtha by a policy of methodically capturing his fortresses one by one and subduing the surrounding countryside. It was a painstaking, unglamorous but highly effective campaign. Marius did his best to undermine it by suggesting both to the soldiery and to his political friends in Rome that he could do the job in half the time if given command of operations. Perhaps he felt that by making a nuisance of himself in this way, Metellus would release him from his position as legate and allow him to stand for the consulship in Rome. (Command of major campaigns usually went to serving consuls or ex-consuls). However, the idea of having the bumptious and openly ambitious Marius as leader of the Republic had little appeal to the refined Metellus. In any case Metellus had been infuriated by the fact that Marius had organized the prosecution – for treason – of one of Metellus' clients. This man, like Marius, was serving in the army, and was therefore considered by Marius as a rival. The prosecution was successful and a court martial found Metellus' client guilty. Metellus was forced to condemn his own man to death – on charges that were later found to be false. When that information came out, Plutarch tells us that 'almost everybody sympathized with Metellus in his grief, but Marius, was full of joy. He proclaimed that the condemnation was his own handiwork, and unabashedly announced that he had forced upon Metellus the guilt of sentencing his own man unjustly to death'.[5]

Under the circumstances, Metellus could be forgiven for making life as difficult for Marius as he could. His first reaction to the proposal that Marius wanted to be consul was to mockingly suggest that Marius should wait until his son, Quintus Caecilius Metellus (who was later to gain the *cognomen* of 'Pius'), was old enough to stand as a candidate on the same ballot. Since that was due to happen in around twenty years' time, Marius was unimpressed. He was equally unimpressed when Metellus did give him leave from the army to campaign in Rome. His commander had timed things carefully. By giving Marius leave to go, Metellus was shot of his turbulent legate, which doubtless came as a relief. By releasing that legate when he did, Metellus gave Marius just twelve days to leave Africa, sail to Rome, conduct an election campaign and get elected.

Thanks to a favourable wind, carefully prepared transport, and agents and proxies who had been already campaigning hard for him in Rome, that is exactly what Marius did. His propagandists had told the Roman people that Metellus' careful, stolid campaign was in fact designed by Metellus to prolong the war for Metellus' own profit and glory. This was grossly unfair, but given the recent performance of Roman aristocratic generals, it was also highly credible. If put in charge of the army, announced Marius, he would bring the war to a speedy conclusion and bring the troops home forthwith. This again was grossly unfair, as Marius knew that Metellus had already pretty much got the war won and the troops would be coming home in any case. But the people did not know that.

The senate did, and its members were as unimpressed with Marius the would-be consul as they had been with Marius the tribune. They decided to use their prerogative to keep Metellus in his command in Africa and assign Marius consular duties elsewhere (in Hades would have been the first choice, had there been a way to get him there). Marius had foreseen this measure also. Once he was elected consul he arranged for a friendly tribune to propose that command of the African war be transferred to Marius by law. This was both legal and had precedent dating back to 131 BC and before then to the Second Punic War. Metellus was replaced and Marius got his army – furthermore, as will be seen, it gave Marius a technique for gaining control of an army he was to re-attempt to apply in 88 BC with disastrous consequences.

Now, in 108 BC, the senate showed its disgust with Marius' conduct by awarding Metellus a triumph on his return. He was also awarded an honorary cognomen, and would henceforth be known as Quintus Metellus Numidicus. This latter honour made clear whom the senate felt had won the war, and was a shrewd blow aimed with full appreciation of the wide streak of jealousy running through Marius' character. Another relatively petty measure was to force on Marius a subordinate he was certain to dislike. This was a man called Lucius Cornelius Sulla, a man as drunken and dissolute as they come, but an aristocrat through and through.

These two events – the overturning of a senatorial command by a popular law, and the bringing together of Sulla and Marius – seemed not particularly extraordinary at the time. However, they established the fault lines along which the Roman Republic would later be ripped apart. But until the cataclysm actually came, no one paid much attention. There was a lot else going on. First there was the African war itself. While still in Italy Marius merrily stirred the pot of controversy further. He announced in speeches that he was the true spiritual heir of the old Roman nobility, since like them, he had won his position 'because of his deeds, not because of his ancestors'. He announced – probably with some truth – that the Romans of old would be heartily ashamed of what their descendants had become. Then, when taking his army to war, Marius – contrary to law and custom – recruited men who failed to meet the basic property qualifications for membership of the legions.

It is probable that there was good reason for this. The African wars had been spectacularly unprofitable for the men who actually fought them, and no doubt disillusioned veterans of previous campaigns had passed their impressions on to potential members of the current levy. If there was a shortage of recruits, it is doubtful if the senate did anything to help Marius out of his predicament, so Marius doubtless felt justified in taking men from the Roman commons where his support was strongest. After all, when the state was desperate for men to fight in the Spanish wars, the doubtful qualifications of many a strapping young recruit had been carefully not examined. This move raised a few eyebrows at the time, but no one noted the wider implications – that once they had completed their time of service, these men would have no smallholdings to go home to, and they might look to their general to provide for their retirement. Two decades later this would be a major issue, which further destabilized what had become a wildly unstable republic.

Contrary to precedent, Metellus did not stay to welcome the army's new commander, but left directly for Rome – not that Marius minded much. He threw himself energetically into delivering the results that he had promised the Roman people. Jugurtha meanwhile had allied himself with his father-in-law, Bocchus, the king of Mauretania. By now, thanks to successes under Metellus, the Roman army had higher morale and was getting better at dealing with Jugurtha's guerilla tactics. Under Marius' highly competent leadership the Romans speedily drove Jugurtha from his last citadels in Numidia. Some rough handling quickly persuaded Bocchus to bow out of the war. His diplomats made peace with the Romans. According to that peace, Bocchus would receive part of Jugurtha's former kingdom on condition that he handed over the person of Jugurtha himself.

This handover required some care. If too large a contingent of Romans showed up to collect him, Jugurtha might make a run for it. Too small a contingent, and Bocchus might not feel confident of taking Jugurtha into custody and instead betray the Romans to Jugurtha and his substantial bodyguard. Marius felt he had the perfect solution to this conundrum. The senate had wished Lucius Cornelius Sulla upon him. Excellent. He would get the dissolute scion of the nobility to shove his head into the lion's mouth by ordering him to go to Bocchus and collect Jugurtha. If Sulla did come back with Jugurtha as a prisoner, then Marius would have the war won at a stroke. If Sulla did not come back with Jugurtha, he was very probably not going to come back at all – a less satisfactory outcome, but pretty satisfying anyway. Marius disliked Sulla for several reasons. Firstly Marius was a somewhat prudish minor aristocrat from Arpinum who boasted of his ignorance of foppish Greek literature. Sulla was a well-educated blue-blood who exhibited (in Plutarch's words) 'a diseased propensity to amorous indulgence and an unrestrained voluptuousness from which he did not refrain'.[6]

The historian Sallust fleshes out this character sketch of Sulla.

He was well versed both in Greek and Roman literature, and had a truly remarkable mind. He was devoted to pleasure but more devoted to glory. He never allowed his debaucheries to interfere with his duties (apart from his duties as a husband) but he devoted all his leisure time to them. He was both eloquent and clever, and he made friends easily. When it came to hiding his intentions, his mind was incredibly unfathomable, yet with all else he was extremely generous; especially with money.

Sallust, *The Jugurthine War* 95

Anyway, Marius had a jealous nature, and it stung that the ambassadors from Bocchus preferred the company of Sulla to his own. These ambassadors might have been looking to the long term, knowing that consuls held office only for a year, but the power of the Roman nobility (as represented by Sulla) was entrenched and permanent. It may also have been that Sulla was simply a more convivial host. Therefore, reasoned Marius, if Sulla and the Mauretanians liked each other so much, then they should be allowed to enjoy each other's company a bit more. Nor was Sulla averse to the plan. Indeed, according to some later sources it was he who suggested it. This should have given Marius pause, but the opportunity of either getting Jugurtha or getting shot of Sulla was too great to pass up. Besides, someone had to attempt the suicide mission, so why not Sulla? Having made his case to himself, Marius issued his orders. Sulla was sent with one Aulus Manlius as a delegate to Bocchus.

The mission proved that being decadent and debauched did not prevent Sulla from having nerves of steel, nor the ability to take shrewd gambles with the resolve to follow them through. In disguise the pair of ambassadors slipped past the patrols that the suspicious Jugurtha had set up for the express purpose of preventing contact between Bocchus and the Romans, and thereafter presented their case to the Mauretanian king. Bocchus wavered for some time between handing Sulla and Manlius over to Jugurtha or Jugurtha over to Manlius and Sulla, but in the end Sulla's eloquence won the day. Sulla got Jugurtha as his captive, and Marius had the African war won at a stroke. The events surrounding the capture of Jugurtha set in motion events far more consequential. Firstly, Marius was deeply irked that although he had won the war, the Roman nobility made much of the fact that it was one of their own who had actually effected the capture of Jugurtha. Secondly, and much more importantly, the Roman people decided that Marius' exemplary generalship made him uniquely qualified to lead the state in its hour of peril. For Rome now faced a danger that made the African war look like the sideshow it was. In the north, the barbarians were coming.

Our interest in the African War has been not so much in the war itself, but because this war illustrated both the venality of the Roman nobility and brought about the first meeting of Sulla and Marius. Likewise our interest in the Cimbric Wars is not in the wars themselves, but in how these wars forwarded the rivalry of Marius and Sulla and set back the coming cataclysm of the Italian revolt. Nevertheless, some background is needed.

For all that they originated somewhere in what is Denmark today, the barbarian horde called the Cimbri were a Germanic people. From the Roman perspective, the two key things about the Cimbri were firstly that they were very good fighters, and secondly that there were a great many of them – by modern estimates somewhere around a quarter of a million in all. It is uncertain what started this huge migration from Cimbri's home in the Jutland peninsula (their own legends spoke of rising waters that covered their lands), but by the time they bumped against the Roman frontier, the tribe had been on the move for at least a decade, wreaking havoc in its slow progress through central Europe. By now this huge mass of warlike humanity consisted of at least four major groups; the Cimbri themselves, the Teutones, and the opportunistic Ambrones and Tigurni tribes who were hitching along for the ride.

The Germans became a threat to tribes allied to Rome once they crossed the Danube, and in 113 BC one of these tribes called on Rome for help. The reaction of the Roman commander was pretty much typical and explains why not only the Italians but also the common people of Rome loathed the aristocracy. The aristocrat in charge on this occasion was a treacherous incompetent called Papirius Carbo. On hearing of the incursion, he ordered the Germans to leave the area forthwith. Perhaps to Carbo's surprise, the Germans dutifully agreed, and negotiated a peaceful departure. Treacherously, Carbo set up an ambush to wipe out the tribesmen as they left. Incompetently, he failed to conceal his intentions. The furious Germans promptly wiped out Carbo's army in a battle at Noreia.

From there the Germanic bulldozer moved west, flattening the army of Junius Silanus in Transalpine Gaul in 209 BC and the army of Cassius Longinus at Burdigala in the same year. Two years later the Tigurni took on another Roman army in an independent effort and again won easily. This unbroken string of defeats was due mostly to bad generalship and proved yet again Marius' contention that the contemporary Roman nobility were a disgrace to their ancestors. But it does provide some excuse for the conduct of generals such as Bestia in Africa. In comparison with the Germanic threat, the African war was literally a sideshow. Bestia and his colleagues might have argued that their appeasement of Jugurtha was not because of the latter's massive bribes (or at least not only for that reason), but also because Jugurtha could wait, and the threat from the north could not. Therefore, rather than waste men and resources in Africa, it was better to close off that war on whatever terms and leave Jugurtha until after Rome had seen off the Germans.

While a viable excuse, this fails to explain why even after Marius had brought the African war to a triumphant conclusion, the Romans continued to make a pig's ear out of the Germanic campaign. The ending of the African war meant that in 105 BC Rome was able to put together a massive army of some 80,000 men to deal with the Cimbri. This was the largest single Roman army to take the field since the battle of Cannae in 216 BC in the Hannibalic war. The Cimbri (a term that is generally used as shorthand for both the Cimbri and their allies), fought in primitive tribal groups. Rome's legions had better weapons and armour, a superior logistical system and greater tactical ability. Unfortunately they also had two particularly bone-headed commanders.

One of these men, Mallius Maximus, was of a non-consular family, and was therefore despised by the other commander, highly bred Servilius Caepio. Relations between the two generals were so poisonous that the men under their command camped separately. When the Cimbri approached, the Romans were on the border of the province of Transalpine Gaul near the town of Arausio on the Rhone. It appears that Mallius opened negotiations with the Cimbri without consulting Caepio, and Caepio launched a surprise attack on the Cimbri without telling Mallius. So instead of a combined army of 80,000 Romans acting together, the Cimbri had to cope with two rather confused armies of 40,000 men acting separately, and the Cimbri coped rather easily. The biggest Roman army since the battle of Cannae suffered the greatest Roman defeat since the battle of Cannae. Almost all of the 80,000 strong army were killed. Two notable survivors were the generals Caepio and Mallius who both fled from the battlefield.

With yet another of its armies wiped out, the Roman state was both exhausted and defenceless. All that saved Italy from invasion and sack that year was the fact that it was late in the campaigning season, and the Cimbri did not fancy tackling the Alps in autumn. Instead, they turned off towards

Iberia, giving the Romans valuable time in which to regroup before the enemy returned. Once Rome had mustered enough of an army to have a sporting chance of fighting off the Cimbri, it surprised no one that the Roman people were vehemently opposed to putting a Roman noble in charge of it. In fact, now that a prospective German invasion of Italy had put their necks on the line, the Roman nobility were inclined to agree. So instead of promoting another highly bred idiot, the state turned for salvation to Caius Marius.

Marius rose to the occasion. The changes made to the army in this period are now known as 'the Marian reforms', but in fact many of these reforms had been introduced by Marius' predecessors or represented trends already evolving in the Roman military system. However, Marius certainly deserves the credit for hastening and systematizing these changes. The first of these changes was probably the result of experience in the Jugurthan war. The Romans discovered that chasing the highly mobile Numidians was fruitless with the army as it was currently constituted. So Roman flying columns developed the habit of loading onto individual soldiers much of the kit formerly carried on the baggage train. Now a Roman soldier went to war loaded down with some 60 pounds (27kg) of equipment, including rations, weapons and entrenching tools.

While fighting in Africa and Spain, the Romans had found that small flexible handfuls of men made the best formations. However these 'handfuls' ('maniples' in Latin) were easily overwhelmed by a mass of barbarians. So the Roman legion adopted the cohort, a unit of 480 men. The cohort was not a total innovation – it certainly existed in the Roman army prior to 105 BC – but Marius may have been responsible for making this the standard tactical unit. There were six centuries in a cohort (despite the name, a 'century' contained around eighty fighting men) apart from the First Cohort, which was double-strength. The larger cohort allowed a legion to be more flexible than a phalanx, but the individual components now maintained their internal integrity better under pressure than had maniples. Also at about this time – though it is uncertain how the implementation happened – the legions abandoned other animal totems to give primacy to the eagle.

Having re-arranged his army, the next thing Marius did was to take advantage of the Cimbri's temporary absence to train it. Previously, training in the Roman legions had been a rather hit-and-miss affair with individual commanders training their men as they thought the situation required. The situation now required highly trained and disciplined soldiers, so Marius adopted the technique first thought up by Metellus' second-in-command in Africa, and started training his men like gladiators. This rigorous regime, which emphasized stamina, was constantly maintained throughout a soldier's period of enrolment, and kept the troops at a constant high level of fitness and discipline. Naturally, both since the salvation of Italy made this necessary, and because no Roman commander would imagine doing otherwise, the Italian allies were organized in the same manner and trained with the same techniques.

In fact the 'Marian reforms' formed the basis for the organization of the Roman army for at least the next three hundred years, during which time the bulk of the Roman empire was conquered and the only force in Europe capable of beating the legions was a force composed of other legions. So when the Cimbri resumed their assault on Italy, Marius and his army were ready for them. Rome had been fortunate in getting an extended period of grace, for after the decisive defeat of the Romans at Arausio the Cimbric army had split up and devoted itself to plundering Iberia and Gaul. As they waited for the Cimbri to resume their assault on Italy, the Roman people showed their faith in Marius by electing him consul year after year.

One of Marius subordinates in 104 and 103 was Cornelius Sulla, who repeated his African success by capturing a renegade Gallic king. This rubbed salt into the wounds of Marius who was already jealous that Sulla sported a ring showing the capture of Jugurtha. According to Plutarch, 'Marius, irritated by his [Sulla's] successes, denied him further opportunity for action and blocked his chances of advancement.'[7] Therefore, by the time of the return of the Cimbri, Sulla had transferred to the command of Marius' consular colleague Lutatius Catulus. Under Catulus, Sulla fought a brisk and successful campaign against alpine tribesmen and then forced the tribesmen to supply Catulus' army with provisions so abundant that there was a surplus for Marius and his men. Far from being grateful for his former subordinate's bounty, the jealous Marius was said to have been thoroughly annoyed by it. Sulla may have still been working in his quartermaster's role when the first clash came with the returning Cimbri. Marius defeated them handily in Gaul, but Catulus suffered a setback in Italy when his men refused to fight from the admittedly poor position into which their general had manoeuvred them. Consequently Catulus was forced to retreat beyond the river Po and to wait for Marius to reinforce him.

The combined Roman armies met the Cimbri near Piedmont in northern Italy in 101 BC. The decisive clash was at Vercellae in what is sometimes called the Battle of the Raudine Plain. It was a hot summer day, and the tens of thousands of men advancing into battle stirred up such great clouds of dust that visibility was limited. This caused some embarrassment to Marius as he led his portion of the army at high speed into the dust cloud. Because the enemy had – quite logically – concentrated their forces on Catulus' men, Marius missed the Cimbric army altogether. So while Catulus engaged the barbarians in a pitched battle, Marius spent some time marching back and forth through the dust cloud in an attempt to work out where the event was taking place. By the time he arrived, the barbarians had been broken. Much of the victory was due to a brilliantly timed cavalry charge that broke the Cimbric cavalry and drove it back onto the ranks of the infantry just as they were deploying. It is quite possible that it was Sulla who led the cavalry, though when Plutarch quotes from Sulla's now lost memoirs, we hear only that Sulla reports himself as being in the thick of the action – in marked contrast to the absent Marius.

It is rather typical of Marius that once Rome had been saved from the barbarian horde, the aftermath of the victory passed not in joyous celebration but in a puerile spat over who deserved the most credit. Marius tried to claim all the kudos for the victory for himself, but Catulus took impartial observers from the city of Parma to the battlefield and showed them the bodies. Many Cimbri still had embedded in their corpses the pilums that had killed them, and the vast majority of these pilums carried the markings of Catulus' legionaries. (This is incidentally the only indication we have that pilums were so marked.) As a result the victory at Vercellae was celebrated by the joint triumph of both generals in Rome. As overall commander and as the victor of previous engagements, Marius received the most praise. Nevertheless, it rankled with him that Catulus and Sulla had actually won the final battle for Rome, and so stolen some of the glory that Marius felt should rightly have been his. He never forgave either man.

Chapter 3

The State of Italy

F aced with imminent disaster from an external threat, the peoples of the Italian peninsula had pulled together to overcome the crisis. With the barbarians so decisively defeated that the only Cimbri remaining in Italy were tens of thousands of enslaved captives, the non-Romans of Italy turned their attention to their next problem – the Romans of Italy. The self-inflicted disaster that hit Rome in 91 BC could have been rectified with relative ease had the Romans acted decisively a decade earlier. Politically speaking, the situation then was rather close to the way it had been three decades earlier. Almost no progress had been made in the enfranchisement of the Italians since the death of Gaius Gracchus in 121 BC. As one historian gloomily remarks, 'The period was one of depression, when flaws in the fabric of the state were made uncomfortably plain, yet nothing worth the mention was done to repair them.'[1]

However, 'almost no progress' does not mean 'no progress'. The Roman oligarchy had so disgraced itself in the last years of the second century BC that some public backlash was inevitable. For the provincials, the significant part of that backlash was a measure passed in around 104 BC called the *Lex de rebus repetudis*. By this law a provincial administrator could be indicted and forced to return any monies he had received from illegal activity, even if he had not directly participated in the illegal activity. Admittedly, the Roman people passed this law more out of spite against the senate than for consideration for the provincials, but it provided some relief nevertheless. Also it was encouraging that a successful prosecution would be rewarded by the grant of Roman citizenship to those who brought the suit.

This gesture towards foreigners was partly because once Marius returned to Rome he became involved in politics. Since the optimates remained more than cool toward him, Marius strove to maintain the support of the masses. Since the common people of Rome still fondly remembered the Gracchi, Marius' allies and policies had a somewhat Gracchan bent. The hopes of non-Roman Italians were further raised by the fact that Marius unilaterally gave Roman citizenship to a thousand men of Camerinum who had fought particularly well for him. When reproached for this illegal action, Marius did not back down but replied that the 'din of battle had overwhelmed the sound of legalism'. Furthermore, when Marius started looking for land for his veterans once the legions were stood down, his proposed colonies had not only Roman citizens, but also holders of the Latin Right (p.20), which indicates that a number of Italian veterans had been put on the fast track to citizenship.

However, even though on the ropes, the cunning and unscrupulousness of the optimates meant that they should never be underestimated. The most scrupulous of the bunch, Metellus Numidicus was exiled for refusing to swear an oath to obey a Marian-sponsored law that none of his fellow senators had any intention of obeying anyway, but his exile marked the low point of optimate political weakness. The sympathy shown by the Marians to the Italians – scant as it was – was used by the optimates to turn the Roman mob against Marius' allies, while Marius himself also had either to distance himself from these men or appear to endorse the thuggery and occasional murder by which those allies held power. Eventually the senate felt strong enough to outlaw the most extreme of the 'Gracchan' demagogues who were thereafter stoned to death by a mob incited and led by optimates. Marius wisely decided to leave town, suddenly recalling an oath he had made to visit Asia Minor.

The optimates were back in power and on a roll. They had Metellus Numidicus recalled from exile with barely a murmur of opposition. Then, given that Italy seemed peaceful, the senate decided to push its luck a little further. The Italians and other non-Romans had played some part in public disturbances during the Marian supremacy in Rome. Though they lacked a vote, they had been numerous enough to pack legislative meetings of Roman voters and make their feelings clear through heckling or downright intimidation. This was considered unwarranted interference in the affairs of the Roman people, so the consuls of 95 BC passed a law ordering the expulsion of all Latins and Italians resident in Rome. They also ordered those censors taking the next census to rigorously inspect the Roman citizenship of any Italian with suspect grounds for claiming it.

This law – the *Lex Licinia Mucia* – was an insensitive misjudgement, for it
not only outraged the thousands of non-Romans who had made their homes
on the seven hills, but it had a symbolic value that was clear to all Italians.
Despite their shared sacrifice in the African and Cimbric wars, the Roman
government had spelled out, as clearly and unambiguously as possible, that
the Italians were not welcome. They were good enough to fight and die
alongside Roman legionaries in wars declared by and for the good of Rome,
but in all other respects the Italians were not even second-class citizens.
Cicero was a youth when this law which sowed the wind was passed, but a
young man when Rome reaped the subsequent whirlwind. His opinion was
unambiguous and bitter – 'to ban foreigners from a city is inhumane' he
said,[2] adding:

> Though it was passed by two consuls who were the wisest of all, I
> observe that everyone agrees that the *Lex Licinia Mucia* was not only
> pointless but destructive. … the feelings of the Italian peoples were so
> alienated by this law that it was the main cause of the war which broke
> out three years later.
>
> Asconius 67–8C

If the Roman senate had proposed the *Lex Licinia Mucia* with the express
purpose of uniting the Italians against Rome, they could hardly have done
a better job. Resentment in the peninsula rose from simmering to boiling
point. The Italian people were a diverse lot, but resentment of Rome in all its
facets gave them common ground. Furthermore the leaders of the Italians
were linked by the bonds of guest-friendship (*hospitium*), which joined most
of the aristocrats of ancient Italy. *Hospitium* meant more than providing for
the needs of an aristocratic traveller when he passed through the lands of
another aristocrat, for once *hospitium* was established, the parties would
work to represent the other's interests in their community and, naturally
enough reciprocate the hospitality in a return visit. In short, *hospitium* meant
that Italy's leaders had already a social old-boy network in place, and with
the provocation of the *Lex Licinia Mucia* this network evolved from a social
organization to the prototype command structure of an Italian rebellion.

It is highly probable that the leaders of the Italian people had previously discussed the possibility they might unite in rebellion against Rome, but conversation now turned from theoretical after-dinner discussions to highly practical planning sessions. It is now time to turn to the issues that would have been discussed at these sessions. Uniting the Italians against Rome would not be easy, for hostility to Rome was about all the Italians had in common.

Ethnically, linguistically and culturally the peoples of Italy were as diverse as the climate and geography of the peninsula they shared. Just under 30 per cent of the landmass of Italy is mountainous, with the Alps running across the north and the Apennine mountain range extending over 1,300km (800 miles) from north to south to split the peninsula in two. The Apennines just east of Rome spread from east to west across 190km of the peninsula – which is only 240km at its widest. Even the Apennines were diverse. The northern portion was thickly forested on its lower slopes and supported large flocks of sheep and goats even where the more fertile valleys had not been cleared for farming. But as one moves southward the land became drier and more barren, with dusty plateaus and high mountains containing few natural resources and fewer inhabitants.

The two-thirds of Italy that was not mountain ranges consisted of terrain that varied from marshes, especially the Pontine Marshes and the marshes of Etruria; lakes of which there were over a thousand, with the Lacus Benacus (Lake Garda) being the largest; high, barren alpine plateaus, and forests and dense scrubland that covered much of the remainder of the peninsula. At a very rough estimate, less than 15 per cent of first century Italy was farmland, and many of these farms were hidden in small valleys or tucked away alongside coastal enclaves – hard to get to and barely worth the journey once one did. The most fertile farmlands in Italy lay (and still lie) along the banks of the River Po in the plain which lies between the northern end of the Apennines and the southern foothills of the Alps. So difficult did the Apennine range make travel to the region that in imperial times Rome found it easier to import grain from Egypt than from the farmlands of the Po Valley.

At the other end of the Apennines was Apulia, the heel of the 'boot' shape of Italy. Apulia was another patch of rich farming land that was hard to reach by land, since mountains blocked off Apulia from the land side and many of the sea approaches ended in sheer cliffs. Therefore the fertile region from which Rome drew its local resources consisted of Italy's western uplands and plains. These stretched from the foothills of the Alps in the east down through Etruria and past Rome to Campania in the south. This region comprised the Roman heartland – the chunk of Italy that Rome would have to hold at all costs if it were to survive. Apples, olives and cereals all grew well here, but even at this relatively early stage in the city's development, the urban mass of Rome consumed more than this region could supply. Grain had to be imported from Sicily and increasingly from the new colony on the site of Carthage in Africa.

To pre-imperial Romans, Italy was a geographical description and not a nation. That geography meant that parts of Italy were harder to get to than places abroad hundreds of miles further away. And – as would-be conquerors from Pyrrhus to the Allies of World War II have discovered – the Italian terrain is eminently defensible. Consequently Greece and Egypt were integrated into the Roman empire before the last bits of Italy officially became Roman. (Egypt was conquered in 32 BC, while some Alpine tribes were still resisting the legions in 6 BC.)

In fact as far as the Romans of the early first century BC were concerned, the northern bit of the peninsula was not Italy at all. It was a part of Gaul. To be precise, it was Cisalpine Gaul – 'Gaul this side of the Alps' – a region so wild and woolly that it was only organized as a proper Roman province in 81 BC, at the end of the decade described in the following chapters of this book.

As the name suggests, the population of Gallia Transalpina was largely Celtic, consisting of the Insubres and the Ligurians in the west and the Veneti in the east. None of these tribes had any great fondness for Rome. The Romans had occupied the Insubrian capital of Milan in 221 and the tribesmen had responded by allying with the Carthaginians in the Hannibalic war. For the last century the Insubres had been reluctant allies of the Romans, which is more than could be said for the Ligurians. They too allied with the Carthaginians, but they didn't stop fighting when Hannibal did. Liguria lay across the land route to Hispania, and the Romans had built the via Aurelia across Ligurian land so that they could reach Hispania at any time of the year. Naturally enough, the Romans wanted to keep the road they had built under their control, while the Ligurians did not want the Romans there at any price. The result was another eighty years of sporadic warfare, which only came to an end around the time of the Cimbric invasion.

North-eastern Italy was occupied by the Veneti. Fragments of their language found on inscriptions show strong Latin influence, but this may have been cultural rather than genetic – the people were probably ethnically close to the Illyrian tribes who lived along the Adriatic. Being habitual foes of the Insubres, the Veneti allied with the Romans in the Hannibalic war mainly because the Insubres chose the other side. The grateful Romans responded by colonizing the area without going through the usual preliminary stage of conquest. Aquileia was founded in 161, and the ancient city of Patavium (Padua) was increasingly Romanized. (The historian Livy later came from here.) By the mid-90s BC the Veneti were clearly not allies of the Romans, but subjects.

As we move south, the east side of the Apennines changes from Transpadene Gaul to Roman Picenum. The area had been Roman since 240 when the local Senones tribe had been conquered and summarily ejected from all but a land-locked area around their capital, Asculum. Not unexpectedly, Picenum had subsequently sided with Rome against Hannibal. Allegiance in the Hannibalic war appears to have been something of a litmus test for events of a century later, because many of the areas that sided with Hannibal tended to also be anti-Roman a century later, while those sides that stuck with Rome through the Hannibalic war could generally be counted on not to rebel, or at least to do so reluctantly. Therefore those plotting rebellion in the mid-90s BC probably knew that Picenum would remain pro-Roman – Asculum and its environs however, were a completely different matter.

Over the Apennines south-west of Picenum was Etruria. This area had been dominated by the Etruscan culture in previous centuries, but by the first century BC Roman influence was so strong that Etruscan was a dying language and the region was almost entirely assimilated by Rome. This region was of considerable strategic significance – not only was the agriculture of the region vital to Rome, but the Etruscans had built solidly, and cities such as Volterrae were massively fortified obstacles to any invader. Suborning the loyalty to Rome of the inhabitants of these cities was the easiest way of conquering them, and something that the would-be rebels of the embryonic Italian confederacy certainly contemplated.

Just south of Etruria and still on the western side of the Apennines lay Latium. This area was the home of the Latins, the people from whom Rome had arisen to conquer most of the known world. The problem was that in terms of area, Latium was tiny in comparison to the rest of Italy. A determined man could ride right across the place in a day, especially given the abundance of local roads which led to Rome. This fact was particularly worrisome to any Roman of a thoughtful disposition, for not much more than a day's march east of Rome were peoples whose loyalty was beyond doubt non-existent. The north-east was less of a problem, because Umbria was sparsely populated and much of that population lived in colonies that Rome had founded – less out of worry about the local Umbrians than from concerns about Gauls invading southward through the region. We shall come to the military role of Roman colonies in due course.

South-east of Rome lived a different kind of Umbrian – the Samnites. It tells us much of what we need to know about the Samnites that they were one of the earliest types of gladiator to fight in Roman arenas. This stubborn and ferocious people had disliked the Romans since they had first met them in the fourth century BC, and first century Romans still smarted from the humiliation of the defeats inflicted by the Samnites at the Caudine Forks in 321 BC and Lautulae in 315 BC. Fighting along the valley of the River Liris was particularly intense, and the Samnites proved astute diplomats as well as fighters. At various times they successfully roped both Gauls and Etruscans into the anti-Roman cause. However, those fighting the Romans gradually buckled under their opponents' tenacity and superior organization. In 291 the Romans captured the Samnite city of Venusia, temporarily bringing Samnite opposition to an end.

The Samnites remained subdued for almost a decade, until the arrival in Italy of Pyrrhus the would-be Epirote conqueror. The Samnites enthusiastically joined Pyrrhus and provided some of the manpower lost in his infamous Pyrrhic victories. One of these victories was at Asculum, a city that was to play a large part in subsequent events. When Pyrrhus was forced to withdraw, the Romans again settled accounts with the Samnites, and forced them to submit after a short but painful war. Thereafter, no one was surprised when the Samnites were among the first to welcome Hannibal to Italy and among the last to abandon his cause once he left the peninsula.

For the century thereafter the Samnites had been resentful allies of Rome, paying taxes and contributing manpower to the Roman armies. No one doubted for a moment that, given the ghost of a chance, the Samnites would rise again. Samnite country was about a week's march from the centre of Rome, something that one might imagine the senate would factor into its geopolitical calculations, but which it inexplicably appears to have failed to do.

Then there were the Marsi – a people closely related to the Samnites, except that they were somewhat more ferocious and lived even closer to Rome. By and large the Marsi lived peacefully with their Roman neighbours. The Marsi were deeply annoyed in 301 BC by the foundation of the Roman colony of Carsoli on their borders, and it took a brisk war to make them accept the imposition. Thereafter the Marsi were steadfast allies of Rome, and refused to submit to Hannibal despite his violent attacks on their territory. The historian Appian says that Rome had celebrated 'no triumph over the Marsi, and no triumph without them',[3] which shows how tightly the Marsi were integrated with the Roman army. The loyalty of the Marsi was taken for granted, even by those Roman senators who helped themselves to Marsic land because it was so conveniently close to Rome. In retrospect, this was a mistake.

Southern Italy consisted of Campania, Bruttium and Apulia, these being the ankle, toe and heel respectively of the Italian boot. Campania, famous for its cavalry, had been an early conquest of the Romans. The Campanians had originally believed that the Romans came to the area to drive out the Samnites who were expanding into the eastern coastal plain. They were right about the Romans beating off the Samnites, but wrong to believe that the Romans would go home afterwards. In fact the first part of Rome's famous Appian Way was built in 312 BC with the precise purpose of delivering legionaries to Campania at high speed should the need arise. The need arose again in 298 when Rome decided to defend the Lucanians (in the area just south of Campania) from the Samnites. The Samnites, Etruscans, Gauls and Umbrians promptly joined forces against Rome in a war that saw the Etruscans crushed, the Samnites temporarily subdued and the Appian Way extended south to Lucania.

Unsurprisingly the Lucanians resented falling under Roman sway and joined Pyrrhus when he arrived in 281 BC. Subjugated in 272 BC after Pyrrhus' departure, the Lucanians demonstrated a laudably never-say-die approach by also supporting Hannibal when he arrived in 216 BC. The warring Roman and Carthaginian armies devastated the area, and left a legacy of bitterness against Rome, which meant that should the Italians rise in rebellion, the Lucanians could be counted on to be in the Italian ranks, gamely prepared for round three. From Lucania we move on to decidedly bumpy Bruttium, modern Calabria, the mountainous region in the toe of Italy. The Bruttii were close relatives of the Samnites. They conquered the area in the third century BC and were decidedly bitter about having to cede sovereignty to the Romans when the legions marched in a generation or two later. The Romans were there to punish the Bruttii for assisting Pyrrhus, but they had some hard fighting to do before they subdued the area. Naturally enough, when Hannibal arrived the Romans had to do it all over again, because the Bruttii supported Hannibal right up to his last days in Italy. The Bruttii were severely punished for their allegiance. Roman colonies were placed right across their territory, and Bruttii tribesmen were forbidden to serve with the Roman army. It is not known if this decree was ever rescinded, and their misfortunes had left the Bruttii as a people severely diminished in any case. Nevertheless, if the name of the Bruttii came from the Lucanian word for 'rebel' – and it probably did – then when the time came, rebel against Rome the Bruttii would certainly do once again.

The 'heel' of Italy, Apulia, became Roman in the same way as Lucania and Campania. The Romans arrived to protect the people against the Samnites, and never left. Apulia supported Hannibal, but had little choice in the matter, as it was at Cannae in Apulia that Hannibal came close to defeating Rome itself in 216. However, by then the Romans had already taken the precaution of extending the Appian Way to Brundisium (modern Brindisi) in 264 BC and were consequently able to feed troops into the region and recapture it with relative ease. Nor would Rome easily let go of the region again, as the port of Brundisium became Italy's gateway to Greece and points east in the Republic's growing empire. Those planning rebellion against Rome might get Apulia on the rebel side or at worst warily neutral, but could expect the Romans to try to regain this strategic asset at the first opportunity. Another complicating factor in the south was cities such as Naples, Heraclea and Heraclea, which remained essentially Greek in their culture. No one was quite sure which way this particular cat was going to jump when the rebellion came, but the Romans had hedged their bets by making Naples into a Latin Colony and founding the colony of Neptunia right next to Tarentum.

Overall then even if the Greeks stayed out of the fight, the would-be rebels had cause for optimism. Essentially the Gallic north would probably remain quiescent – less out of sympathy for Rome than because the Gauls had too little in common with the other Italians. Picenum would probably stay loyal, and Umbria too, though Umbria was less certain. Campania and Etruria had been Roman for so long that without yet more provocation from the Roman government it was hard to imagine them joining any revolt. That left everything else west and south of Rome – a fairly contiguous block of land and peoples, all with ancient grudges against the Romans and seething resentment for recent mistreatment. Beyond a doubt, the conspirators assured each other at their clandestine meetings, the South would rise again.

There was just one problem with this happy picture. Rome had carefully inserted a great many flies into the ointment in the form of colonies. A Roman colony was not occupied land cultivated for the benefit of Rome – it was an extension of Rome itself. The people of a colony were Roman citizens, fully entitled to vote in election in Rome if they could be bothered to go there for that purpose, and equally entitled to leave their colony and take up residence in Rome if the desire so took them.[4] However, most Roman colonists were content to remain where they were, because Roman colonies were founded on three main criteria. Firstly, the settlers tended to be former legionaries and their families. Secondly, the land they were settled on tended to be the richest and most fertile lands in the territory the Romans were occupying, and thirdly, even more than rich farmlands, Roman colonies were founded on defensible sites of strategic importance. There were a great many such colonies, because the Romans had a great deal of Italy both to keep down and also to defend. Therefore some colonies were not Roman but Latin, though many volunteers for these settlements were raised from the poor of Rome itself. A Latin colony was different from a *Colonia Civium Romanorum*, and had a different constitution and rights in relation to Rome. However, both

Latin and Roman colonies both had a tendency to grow into flourishing cities and these cities, unlike those of the reluctant allies among whom the colonies were placed, were answerable directly to Rome and owed the city their complete allegiance.

Roman colonies developed as a consequence of the traumatic Latin War, which finished in 338 BC. Before then Rome had looked at the other states of Latium as colleagues in mutual defence. The fact that these states sided with other local tribes against Rome was a sobering experience that convinced the Romans that they needed to look to their own defence. The idea of doing so with military colonies was not a new one. There were plenty of examples from earlier Greek history from which the Romans could learn, though some aspects of the foundation process made Roman writers think that the original inspiration came from the Etruscans.[5]

That these first colonies were primarily defensive is easily determined by their location, which took careful consideration of terrain, both in making the colonies hard to assail, but also giving them command of strategic features such as choke points in land communications. If there was a single land route to any area of Italy, the chances were that a Roman colony lay across that route. These colonies also served the same purpose as any military outpost – to give early notice of enemy activity, and to slow or block it while the main base prepared its response. Because of this primary purpose, Roman colonies were not just founded in lands with surly inhabitants of a distinctly anti-Roman inclination, but even in places that had been Roman for generations but which had strategic locations worth controlling.

Many of the original colonies were Latin colonies, but the Hannibalic war convinced the Romans both of the importance of colonies and the importance of keeping them loyal (the loyalty of the Latin colonies held through the war, but definitely wavered at times). Most colonies after the war were settled by Roman citizens, and these colonies were considerably more substantial than pre-war Roman settlements. Often the colonies were founded on existing sites taken from recently conquered locals, and were renamed to something that the new occupants preferred. For example Malventum, which sounded like 'bad event' to Latin ears, became Beneventum, Nequinum on the river Nar became Narnia, and so on.

Among the more important colonies, Tarracina controlled the land route between Latium and Campania, while Fabrateria Nova blocked the approaches to Latium from the south-east – a job that had been that of the Latin colony of Fregellae until it was flattened for mutiny against Rome in 125. Cremona and Placentia controlled access to Italy from the north-east – which is why in AD 69 two invading Roman rebel armies each fought a separate battle at Cremona. Bononia (modern Bologna) did the same job in guarding the north-west, with well-fortified Mutina (Modena) as support in Cisalpine Gaul. Cosa was a key site in Etruria, and Venusia occupied such a strategic point that the Romans had made it a colony as soon as they captured it from the Samnites in the war of 291. Beneventum was one of a string of colonies that separated the Samnites proper from the Hirpini tribe, while Aesernia and Aufidena did a similar job of keeping the Samnites and Marsi from joining up. In the far south Thurii had the job of controlling the restive Bruttii.

Overall, there were almost a hundred Roman and Latin colonies scattered across strategic locations all over Italy. In later centuries the political commentator Machiavelli considered Roman colonies as the most effective source of Roman strength. Not only did the colonies have a strategic role, but they were also effective instruments of romanization, the process that was later to knit Italy into a unified cultural entity. From the point of view of those plotting rebellion against the power of Rome, the colonies were collectively and individually a royal pain in the neck. They were too numerous and too well-defended to be defeated individually and too well situated to be ignored. And, as it turned out, they were also too loyal to be subverted – apart from one notorious exception, which we will come to later. It is reasonable to claim that without the colonies, Rome might well have lost the approaching war. With the colonies, Roman armies, even those deep in otherwise hostile territory always had a secure base on which to fall back and mountain passes and river crossings were secured for them even as they were denied to the rebels. It was the existence of the Roman colonies as much as any lingering sentiments of moderation that made the Italians of the late 90s BC decide to give peace one last chance. At this time, their hopes that the coming cataclysm might be averted rested on the shoulders of one man – Livius Drusus.

Chapter 4

Livius Drusus, the Failed Reformer

The Roman senate had lost ground in the years before 100 BC. In his struggle with the senate Gaius Gracchus had transferred certain powers from that august body to the class a step lower in Roman society – the equites. The equites are sometimes called the 'middle class' of Rome, which they were not. To use a rough analogy with the modern western world if the 'senators' are the politicians, the equites are the bankers, the share dealers and the CEOs of transnational companies. That is to say, the equites were often immensely rich and thanks to Gracchus, politically powerful as well.

It will be remembered that the *repetundae* courts were set up to punish any Roman magistrate who used his powers to enrich himself – or who took a cut of the profits from anyone else whom that magistrate allowed to illegally exploit Roman subjects. Since many Roman senators dreamed of being given charge of a province to rape financially, the senate was always going to be sympathetic to anyone charged of extortion while in office. Therefore Gracchus gave charge of the *repetundae* courts to jurors from the equites. Regrettably, all this legislation did was to give the equites the chance to prove they could be as greedy, short-sighted and blatantly corrupt as even the senate on a bad day.

The equites finally out-did themselves with the trial of Rutilius Rufus, and so inadvertently set in motion a sequence of events that precipitated the long-brewing Italian revolt. We meet Rutilius Rufus on p.90 as the second-in-command who handed over the African army to Marius in 107 BC. This Rufus was also the man whose training techniques were adopted by Marius and so helped the legions throw back the threat of a Cimbric invasion. Rufus extended his record of public service by serving as legate to the governor of the Roman province of Asia in western Anatolia. The governor, Mucius Scaevola, was an honest man, something so rare that the provincials there long afterwards celebrated festivals in his honour. Scaevola and Rufus cracked down hard on the tax-collectors, slave dealers and other members of the equites who were long accustomed to looting the province with impunity under more complaisant governors. Given such a record, Rufus deserved well of the state he had served so faithfully. However, the Rome of the early first century offered few rewards for honest men.

The wealthy and well-connected Scaevola was seen by the corrupt tax-collectors as too difficult a man to challenge, but Scaevola had returned to Rome after nine months leaving the remainder of his governorship for Rufus to conduct alone. During that time, alleged the equites, Rufus had extorted vast sums from the populace of the province. The charge was so manifestly untrue that no one believed it for a moment. In a way that was exactly the point. The trial in 92 BC was to be a warning to the senate not to interfere with the activities or the equites – or else. Despite his obvious innocence, Rufus was found guilty and ordered to repay the money he had not in fact extorted. Since he had not taken the money Rufus was naturally unable to pay it and was exiled from Rome. He chose to live out his exile in the very province he was accused of looting and was welcomed there as an honoured guest. Turning down later invitations to return to Rome, Rufus lived to the ripe old age of 80, universally respected, and one of the few genuinely good guys of his era.

That the equites unabashedly condemned such a man was unequivocal proof of moral bankruptcy, which briefly united the people and senate of Rome in their distaste. Consequently senate and people worked together to elect as tribune a man who would correct future abuses of this kind. Their choice was Livius Drusus. This Livius Drusus was the son of the man who had out-demagoged Gaius Gracchus in 121 BC (p.22). The people still remembered the older Drusus' land grants fondly, for all that the senate had reneged on putting them into effect. Furthermore the younger Drusus was a man of known honesty and integrity.[1]

Livius Drusus started his year in office with three priorities – to sort out the conflict between the senate and the equites, to resolve the problems of exploitation and misuse of the *ager publicus*, the public land, and to deal with the mutinous discontent of the Italians. As Drusus was well aware, the three issues had to be dealt with simultaneously, for they were deeply interconnected.

For example, reforming the use of the public land would entail more of it being given to Roman citizens. This would displace Italians who still used that land, even though they technically had no right to it. Certainly the Italians had farmed there for generations, but they had lost title to the land after their ancestors had been beaten by the Romans in war. So if the land commissioners started redistributing that land, the Italians would lose out – unless they too were Roman citizens. However, making Roman citizens, and therefore voters out of the Italians would upset the balance of power in Rome, where the aristocracy had generally stitched up the various constituencies of voting tribes through a mixture of bribery, intimidation and patronage. The last thing the senate wanted was hordes of voters flooding in from the countryside. Such rural voters would be hard to intimidate, expensive to bribe and were more easily patronized and bullied by their own aristocracy. Those rural Italian aristocrats would also be Romans once they were enfranchised, and with their own cadres of rural voters they too would be able to stand for public office in Rome. And junior senators felt that those public offices had already too many candidates competing for them.

So public land could not be sorted out without dealing with the Italian issue, and the Italian issue could not be dealt with without sorting out the balance of power in the senate, which could not be resolved while the senate was feuding with the equites. It was a pretty conundrum, and one made even more difficult by the violent impatience of the Italians, the petty self-interest of the senate and the shameless greed of the equites. There were men of goodwill on all sides, but by and large factionalism and intransigence ruled the day. A considerable majority regarded compromise not as statesmanship but weakness, and were determined that all concessions should come from the others. It would take a Solomon to sort out the mess, but Livius Drusus was determined to give it a sporting try.

At this point a caveat must be mentioned by the conscientious historian describing the events that happened next. In the early first century we have something of a hole in the historical record. The ever-dependable chronicle of Livy is missing, no doubt because the Romans of late antiquity had little interest in committing the deplorable events he describes to the highly expensive parchment which would have preserved them for posterity. And with Livy missing, we have no contemporary historian who fills the gap, leaving us with fragments of evidence and the highly abbreviated and sometimes contradictory accounts of the later writers Appian and Velleius Paterculus. Therefore the exact order and details of what Drusus did during his tribunate are lost, though the general outline remains clear. What follows is both a description of that outline and an attempt to flesh out the details without plunging into the minutiae of scholarly controversy that surrounds the topic.

It seems reasonably clear that the first challenge that Drusus had to overcome was the perception that he was the senate's champion. In part it says something about the extent to which Romans accepted the aristocratic capture of public office that no one found it extraordinary that the senate's champion should be a tribune of the plebs. This, despite the fact that the tribune was intended to be the people's champion against the very senate that Drusus was considered to be representing. However, at this point the common people agreed with the senate that the equites needed taking down a peg, so they were happy enough to elect the senate's choice of a man 'most noble, most eloquent, entirely above reproach' to do the taking down.[2] In fact, it was that venerable rogue Aemilius Scaurus, leader of the senate, who first called on Drusus to do this (Scaurus was being tried by the equites for extortion at the time). So having been chosen by senate and people, Drusus would have been aware that the general understanding of his intentions put the equites implacably against him.

The epitomator of Livy is unambiguous about what those intentions actually were, describing Drusus as 'a tribune of the plebs who wanted to reinforce the powers of the senate' (*Epitome* 71). Unfortunately, while the senate wanted a partisan who would fight their corner whether they were right or wrong, and the plebs wanted a scourge for the equites, Drusus wanted to actually put things right. Drusus probably foresaw that this would infuriate everyone but the equites (who didn't count, since they were furious with him already). Nevertheless Drusus rejected the senate and people's role for him and chose to represent a different constituency – the few men of goodwill on all sides who still hoped for a peaceful resolution to the entire ghastly mess. Perhaps Drusus was prepared to face the storm of outrage his actions would cause in the short term because he thought everyone would thank him later, once it was all sorted out.

Once Drusus set to work, the first item on his agenda was the courts. These Drusus certainly sorted out, though no two of our historical sources agree on exactly how, and the details of his *Lex iudiciaria* are now lost. The epitomator of Livy (quoted above) says that Drusus divided juries between senate and equites. Velleius Paterculus says that Drusus restored control of the courts to the senate. Appian agrees, but adds that this was a compromise achieved by doubling the size of the senate to 600 through recruiting 300 of the most influential equites into the senatorial order. Of the various accounts, it would seem that Appian is largely correct, simply because no one liked the law, and the solution described by Appian would certainly succeed in upsetting everybody. The equites would be furious that courts were taken out of their control, because their instrument for keeping governors docile had been wrenched from their hands; the senate was appalled that 300 new rivals had been added to the competition for magistracies; and the people failed to understand how promoting 300 equites to the senate constituted the punishment of that group that they had been looking for. Essentially Drusus had provided a solution to the problem of partisan and unjust courts that the equites certainly did not want and which failed to satisfy the senate and people because they wanted revenge, not solutions. The *Lex iudiciaria* was not popular.

Drusus may have suspected that this would be the case, for he quickly followed up the *Lex iudiciaria* with another law, a *Lex agraria*. This 'land law' was a straightforward measure. It dealt with the colonies that were to have been founded when Drusus' father was trying to outbid Gaius Gracchus for popular support. The proposal to settle some of Rome's population in new colonies had been very popular, but once the senate had defeated Gaius Gracchus, the proposal had quietly been allowed to die. Now Drusus wanted to revive it again, and at the second time around the idea proved to be as popular with the Roman people as it had been when it was first proposed. Furthermore, a series of minor bills were proposed that dealt with exactly what land was to be allocated and how. This was very popular with the Roman people, but much less so with the senate. This was probably because, like Tiberius Gracchus before him, Drusus intended some of that land allocation to come from public land that Roman aristocrats were squatting on illegally. Certainly Philippus, the consul of that year, was vehemently opposed to the *Lex agraria* and did all in his power to block it. This led to what might politely be called some 'robust politics'. For example, on one occasion when Philippus was orating against the proposals in the forum, Drusus went so far as to grab the consul by the throat. He choked the top magistrate in Rome so savagely that blood from a nosebleed flooded down Philippus' chest. Drusus dismissed reproaches of his violent conduct with the contemptuous comment that what had erupted from Philippus was not blood but thrush soup.[3] Philippus had a reputation as a gourmet, while the lifestyle of Drusus was famously austere.

The senate was in a dither as to whether to support their unpopular consul or the unpredictable champion they had chosen in their tribune of the plebs. As we have seen, Drusus was a lot more forceful than his wavering contemporaries. At one point he came close to ordering another senatorial opponent of his measures to be thrown off the Tarpeian rock. This rock, on the Capitoline hill, overlooked a precipitous drop, and it was the Roman practice to throw traitors off it to their doom. Cicero tells a tale that neatly sums up senatorial bemusement at Drusus' activities.

> When a man called Granius met Drusus, Drusus greeted him with 'Quid agis?' [roughly 'What are you up to these days?']. Granius replied 'No by God, Drusus what in the world are you up to?'
>
> Cicero, *pro Plancio* 33

Violent though the opposition to Drusus' reforms might have been in the senate, it was not unanimous. Drusus had his supporters, notably the great orator L. Crassus. Combined with the energetic and forceful Drusus, Crassus and his faction could just about hold the line with the senate, but opposition to the agrarian bill did not end there. Not just senators were illegal squatters on Roman public land. There were also the Italians. In wars of previous centuries the ancestors of these Italians had paid for their defeat with the loss of their land to the Romans (Rome generally took around one-third). However, apart from declaring the confiscated territory Roman public land, in many cases the Romans had done nothing else about it, leaving the land to be farmed by its previous owners, who were now technically squatters. Therefore the news that Drusus planned to dust off long-dormant plans to redistribute this land to the Roman plebs was greeted with as much dismay by the people of Italy as it was with enthusiasm by the people of Rome.

Therefore Philippus and his cronies did not address a wholly hostile audience in their harangues in the forum. There were a goodly number of Italians to cheer him on, especially neighbouring Etrurians and Umbrians who had come to Rome to make their dissatisfaction known. Naturally these Etrurians and Umbrians had no vote – something that incensed them further – but they could make their voices heard with vociferous cheering and heckling of public speakers. When the rough-and-tumble of verbal debate degenerated into rough-and-tumble of the more literal sort, as increasingly became the case, the Italians gave as good as they got. Naturally enough this did little to endear the Roman and Italian in the street to one another, and this further worsened the dilemma faced by Drusus.

He needed the support of senate and people or his legislation would not be ratified. He could control the senate if he had the support of the people, because Rome was still a democracy, and it was the people who actually voted laws into force. However, his land laws were essential to keeping the people of Rome on his side, yet to pass his land laws Drusus would have to mortally offend the Italians. Offending the Italians would be extremely dangerous, for years of delay and the repeated sidelining of their cause had left the peoples of Italy in a dangerously mutinous mood.

As a warning of what was to come. Pompaedius Silo, the leader of the Marsi (see p.47) collected 10,000 men whose land claims would not stand scrutiny by an allocation commission.[4] His plan was to surround the senate house, and demand the citizenship for his people. If the senate refused then the knives would literally be out, for Pompaedius Silo's 10,000 carried weapons concealed under their tunics. What would have happened if this hare-brained plan had actually been executed will never be known, for the marchers were met by a pro-Drusus aristocrat who persuaded them to return to peacefully to their homes.[5] However, it was clear that the patience of the Italians was wearing thin.

Drusus did what he could. There was no way that he could retract his land legislation without losing his credibility and his court reforms as well. However, the Italians needed to be brought onside with the legislation, so Drusus took the dangerous step of promising them the one thing that would appease them. Just let the current legislation go through, Drusus assured the Italian leaders in secret meetings, and once the turmoil had settled the very next item on his agenda would be the grant of citizenship for at least those currently with the Latin Right, and the grant of the Latin Right for all the other Italians. Drusus must have known that what he had promised the Italians would be very hard to sell to the Roman people and senate, but he evidently felt he had no choice but to try. Just to make things even more challenging, just a few days after a splendid speech excoriating the consul Philippus, L. Crassus died. Suddenly, just as Drusus was faced with the greatest legislative challenge of his career, he was deprived of his strongest supporter.

Drusus' popularity with the Roman people waned as suspicions grew that he had done a deal with the Italians. As a man of principle, Drusus had felt bound to warn the consul Philippus that Italian extremists were planning to assassinate him while he was on an excursion to the Alban hills just outside Rome. As a man without principle, Philippus used the warning which had saved his life as a demonstration of how completely Drusus was involved with the most secret plots of the Italians. Desperate to keep his standing with the people, Drusus resorted to bribery; that tried-and-trusted expedient of the aristocracy. He increased the grain dole and decreased both the price and the criteria for eligibility for those who obtained it. This bribe was more than the state could afford, and was paid for only by debasing the silver denarius, the main currency of Rome, by adding an eighth of copper.[6] Thus through bribes Drusus appeased the people but further alienated those economically literate senators who knew their currency was now worth less.

As September approached, the reforming tribune was well aware that he was running out of time. Without Crassus to help in the senate, his legislation was bogged down in an endless series of procedural delays. All the while the support of the common people was ebbing away and Drusus had pretty much run out of things to bribe them with. As he gloomily remarked, he had nothing left to give away but 'air and mud' (the Latin is more poetic – 'air and mud' becomes '*caelum et caenum*').[7] It was time to stake everything on a single throw of the dice. Consequently, Drusus rolled all his planned legislation into one single *Lex* – reasonably enough given how all the various issues were intertwined – with the intention of presenting it to the people to accept or reject for once and for all. Whether or not the people would have accepted the law was problematic. Drusus was nowhere near as popular as he once was, and word of his plans to enfranchise the Italian allies as soon as his legislation had passed seems to have got out. However, plans for Drusus' proposed colonies were still popular, and at least some of the common people fondly remembered their tribune's past benefactions. And of course, there were the Italians, still present in Rome in large numbers and very impatient to get the entire legislative obstacle over with so Drusus could get started on their enfranchisement. Though the Italians had no vote, they would certainly be able to encourage waverers, and block any attempts at interference by thugs of opposing factions.

But in the event, democracy never had its chance. Just the threat that Drusus might still push his legislation through allowed Philippus to unite the senate just enough for a crushing pre-emptive strike. The senate was a consultative rather than a legislative body, and could not vote laws into effect. However, the senate was entitled to express its opinion – in fact that was largely its job – on laws being passed or presented to the people. And the senate ruled that Drusus' entire legislative programme was unconstitutional. This was a devastating blow, because it not only voided the current omnibus law that Drusus wanted the people to vote on, but it also annulled all past legislation that Drusus had already made law. Exactly what justification the senate presented for its action is uncertain, but their main argument seems to have been that Drusus had consistently violated the *Lex Caecilia-Didia* of 98 BC. This law forbade 'tacking' – that is, the adding of extraneous items to a proposed law. So a bill about land reform should not, for example, have items about jury membership included within it. It is possible that Drusus had indeed given hostages to fortune in this way, because he was a young man in a hurry. Back when he was still the senate's champion, he could have merrily tacked extra items onto his legislation, knowing full well that the senate would not challenge them. If so, his earlier haste to get things done now came back to bite him.

Perhaps the knowledge that the senate had him dead to rights explains what Drusus did next. He gave up. He could have kept fighting, because in Republican Rome a tribune had the right to overturn a senatorial decree. But Drusus could do so only by alienating the senate even further, and so dictatorial a step as the use of his veto would also cause unease among the general public who were already wary of his long-term intentions. So, what was the point of trying to do the right thing when the very people you were trying to save fought you every step of the way?

> He chose not to use his power, knowing full well that they [the senators] would soon receive payment in full for their misdeeds. ... Those whose dog-in-the-manger attitude had destroyed his reputation had voluntarily chosen to place themselves at huge risk.
>
> Diodorus Siculus 37.10

For years the Roman Republic had been sliding toward disaster. If we are to pick a single point when the entire crumbling structure lurched past the point of no return, it is probably the moment when the senate voted to undo all that Drusus had done and was trying to achieve. Those present had no idea of the events their vote would set in motion. Within the next decade a huge number of those senators – by some estimates between half and three-quarters – would be dead, and most would have died violently. Ironically this would include Titus Didius. It was his *Lex Caecilia Didia* that was the excuse for the senatorial vote that unleashed the cataclysm. As is often the case with world-shaking events, the fact only became clear with retrospect, though the writer Obsequens (who had perfect hindsight, writing 400 years later) says that the gods did their best to warn the Romans. At Arretium, blood flowed from the loaves as people broke their bread, in Rome the temple of Piety was hit by lightning, and at Cumae the statue of Apollo in the citadel was seen to break into a sweat. Finally (and of great interest to modern Ufologists), at Spoletium, a golden fireball descended to earth, and later took off again heading eastward.[8]

Clearly the gods were trying hard to point out that all was not well, but in Rome at least, no one was listening. As far as the senate were concerned, they had successfully restored the *status quo*. It was left to the survivors and later generations to realize that this was the *status quo ante bellum* ('The way things were before the war'). The Italians were beyond furious. And being of a practical disposition, they prepared to vent their fury in a very practical way. Their leaders had no intention of smashing chairs or vases as an outlet for their temper. Instead they started seriously working to smash the entire Roman state. Therein probably lies the answer to one of the enduring mysteries of the Late Republic. After the failure of his legislation, Drusus withdrew to his house near the Palatine Hill, and seldom ventured out. However, Drusus was still a tribune with administrative duties, and a Roman aristocrat with large estates and swarms of clients seeking his favours. These he attended to within his own house.

> He regularly conducted business in a poorly-lighted cloister. One evening, as he was dismissing his people, he cried out that he had been struck. He fell to the ground, and a cobbler's knife was found thrust into his thigh.
>
> Appian, *Civil Wars* 1.36

The assassination of Livius Drusus remains one of history's whodunnits. The killer took advantage of the general panic and confusion to make his escape. Despite the nice touch of a cobbler's knife (which suggested the killing was by one of the common people, perhaps a disaffected client), we can suspect that the blade was guided by a professional who knew exactly where to find the femoral artery. Wounds to the leg are seldom fatal, but this one was, and almost certainly was intended to be. In asking who was behind the killing we need to look at motive only, since it was the assassin who found the means and the opportunity. Probably we can put aside a personal grudge, as it seems highly coincidental that for centuries Drusus should be the only Roman aristocrat assassinated for personal reasons. If we assume a political motivation, it becomes clear that Drusus was murdered by his friends – the Italian aristocracy.

There was no reason for any Roman senator to want Drusus dead. At this time the senate did not do business that way. Drusus had already been comprehensively defeated, and he had acknowledged the fact. The proper senatorial procedure would be for Drusus to live as long as possible so that he had plenty of time to appreciate his downfall. Maybe in a few years time some up-and-coming aristocrat might make his name by prosecuting Drusus for some imagined crime. Then everyone could get a bit more enjoyment from watching Drusus being packed off into exile. From the senate's point of view Drusus was no threat, and they could only get more sadistic fun out of him if he was alive. The senate played rough but (though this was about to change) the Roman aristocracy sentenced few of their own to death, even for heinous crimes.

The Italians, on the other hand, were well aware that Drusus knew too much. The fact that Drusus had known of their plan to murder the consul Philippus shows his knowledge of the Italians' intimate councils. The Italians had probably repeatedly and very sincerely warned Drusus that they intended to rebel if Drusus failed to get them the franchise. In doing so the Italians intended to give Drusus maximum incentive to achieve their mutual goals. But Drusus had failed, the threat of rebellion now became real and Drusus knew it. He had already warned the consul Philippus of the plan to kill him. Could there be any doubt that Drusus would also warn the senate of Italian plans to destroy the entire state? The last thing that the would-be rebels wanted was the Romans forewarned and forearmed, so for all that he was a friend to the Italians, there was only one way to ensure that Drusus kept silent. Drusus was in the end a Roman and his final loyalty was to Rome. If he lived, he would have had to sound the warning.

Probably all that kept Drusus alive in the brief period after his legislative failure was that he was in frantic secret negotiations with the Italians to avert war, and he was reluctant to betray his friends unless those negotiations failed. The Italians wanted to see if Drusus had anything else to offer, but probably had an assassin already on standby. From the Italian viewpoint, killing Drusus was an act of essential *realpolitik*. The man had failed and was now a danger. Why let him live when they were planning to kill tens of thousands of his compatriots? So with their fatal vote, the senators had not only killed Drusus' legislation and political career, they had also inadvertently killed the man himself. As the coming years demonstrated, many had sentenced themselves to death as well.

Chapter 5

The Breaking Storm

They [the rebels]were completely justified. They wanted to become
citizens of the empire whose lands their arms defended. Every year and
every war they contributed twice the amount of infantry and cavalry [as
the Romans]. And yet they were not allowed to be citizens. It was their
efforts which had raised the state to its pinnacle of success, and yet that
state treated with disdain those of its own race and kin, rejecting them
as strangers and foreigners.

Velleius Paterculus 2.15

W hen the historian Velleius Paterculus describes the struggle of
the Italian people, his heart is clearly on the rebel side. This is
because he was of Campanian stock and it is very probable that
some family members of two generations back were rebels themselves.[1]
Theirs was a cause whose time had come. It is very unlikely that the Italians
waited until the failure of Drusus' legislation before starting preparations
to go to war. It is far more probable that they had been contemplating
rebellion since – as they saw it – the Roman state had declared war on them
with the explicitly anti-Italian legislation of the *Lex Licinia Mucia* of 95 BC
(p.42). Drusus appears to have been the only Roman both perspicacious
enough to realize that fact and to have the power to do something about
it. Because the Italians knew the strength of Rome's armies from a more
intimate perspective than any other peoples, when Drusus offered a credible
alternative to fighting the Italians were more than happy to take it. They
put their plans on hold to see what the reforming tribune could do. When
it turned out that Drusus could not do enough, the Italians picked up their
plotting where they had left off.

The Italian leaders could plan in secret, because making plans simply involved carefully screening those who attended and served at dinner parties. Turning these plans into action was more tricky. There was a cadre of Romans resident in every Italian city. Some had got there by marriage, for most Italians had the *connubium*, the right to marry Romans (though the child took the citizenship of the father). Others had purchased farms or businesses from Italians and now lived in the city where they had made their purchase. Others were people of native stock who had obtained citizenship through service to Rome. This meant that if there were there any actual mobilization of troops, or other overt military preparations, such as strengthening city walls, news was bound to eventually reach the senate. And for all that they had been stupid enough to reject Drusus' proposals, the senators were not so stupid as to assume that the Italians would take this lying down. At the very least, it would be a good idea to check.

Emissaries were dispatched to the cities of Italy to assess the mood of the allies and to note any suspicious activity. Particular attention would have been paid to the tribe of the Marsi. These were a highly warlike people who lived close to Rome, and one of their leaders was Quintus Pompaedius Silo. Silo was a known firebrand, the man who had led his 10,000 protesters to Rome and who had only been dissuaded from violence at the last moment (p.58). Plutarch tells us a story that gives us another glimpse into that man's character.

> While Cato [the younger] was still a boy, the Italian allies of the Romans were trying hard to get the citizenship. One of these was Pompaedius Silo, a war veteran and aristocrat. As a friend of Drusus, he was staying at his house for several days. Becoming friendly with the children, he once asked them 'Come, won't you beg your uncle to help us to get the citizenship?'
>
> Young Caepio smiled and agreed, but Cato remained silent and glared at the foreigners. ... Since the look on his face indicated a plain refusal, Pompaedius Silo held him out of a window and harshly ordered him to agree if he didn't want to be thrown down. He frequently shook the boy as he held him out of the window, which Cato endured without showing panic or fear. Eventually Pompaedius Silo put him down, remarking

quietly to his friends 'Just as well for the Italians that this one is just a boy. If he was a man we'd have lost his vote and everyone else's.'

Plutarch, *Life of Cato the Younger* 2

Silo appears to have been more than one of the Italian leaders. One modern writer refers to him as 'the soul of the whole undertaking'.[2] His later record shows that he was a good commander, skilled in ambush and subterfuge, and as his treatment of the young Cato shows, he was a man who would stop at little to get his way. While he was perhaps the outstanding leader on the Italian side, he was not the only leader. After him in stature among the conspirators was Gaius Aponius Mutilus. Mutilus was a Samnite, and that mountain tribe were ever among Rome's most obdurate enemies whenever circumstances gave them the chance. There were others, including Marius Egnatius, another Samnite who was to be one of the outstanding Italian generals in the first part of the war.

There is a reason why the Italian side had names such as 'Quintus', 'Aponius' and 'Marius', names common, or even renowned, among the Romans. Consider, for example, Marius. Gaius Marius, the Roman who had defeated Jugurtha and the Cimbri came from central Italy, from the very Samnite town of Arpinum (modern Arpino). However, the place was captured by the Romans in 305 BC, and thereafter its people were enrolled as involuntary Roman citizens, since that was how Rome did things at the time. As was usual with citizens acquired through warfare, the people of Arpinum did not have the vote. But this was remedied by 188 BC when it was decided that after almost 120 years of good behaviour the people of the city could be trusted not to do anything rash.

Thus while Arpinum was now a Roman town, nearby Allifae was not, and nor were many others in the neighbourhood. The example of Arpinum shows that whether an Italian city or town was Italian and Roman had little to do with blood or even tribal allegiance, and a lot to do with happenstance, and the vagaries of war and politics. A good rule of thumb in south and central Italy was that the more strategic the location of a settlement, the more likely it was to be Roman, because when the Romans conquered such a location in war they generally refused to give it back. And after a while the population of the occupied city started to think of themselves as Romans as well.

Consequently there were to be no hard and fast battle lines in the coming war. Italians and Romans were too thoroughly intermixed. Many Romans had Italian relatives, and many rural areas had patches of Roman land surrounded by larger areas of Italian land, and vice-versa. Many Italians who got tired of waiting for their Roman citizenship had simply faked it. They could get away with it because the main difference between Roman and Italian was not ethnicity or religion. It was not even language, because by the early first century Latin either supplemented or had supplanted native tongues across much of the central peninsula. The main difference – and in many cases the only difference – between a Roman and an Italian was that one had the vote and the privileges that went with it and the other didn't. The coming war would be as close to a civil war as it could get and would end by actually being one.

We have no exact date for the death of Livius Drusus, but it was probably around October 91 BC. A lot had happened in the year already, but we get no mention of whether Drusus intended to stand for the tribunate the following year, so his death occurred before the electoral meeting of the *comitia centuriata*, but well after the Latin Festival in March at which the Italians had planned to assassinate the consul Philippus. The fact that it was dusk when Drusus was stabbed is suggestive rather than conclusive, for Drusus had a strong work ethic, and could have been working late rather than the dusk coming early. Nevertheless, it is probable that Drusus died in autumn, and the time of the year that the assassination took place is of great importance because it was to determine whether hostilities should kick off in that year – 91 BC – or wait for the start of the following year's campaigning season. (Which was usually in March, the month of Mars.)

Ideally, from the Italian point of view, the Romans should be unaware that anything was amiss while autumn slipped into winter. During the winter, the Italians could hammer out and sign their final diplomatic treaties for military alliances. Hostages could be exchanged, and military targets assigned to each of the rebel groups. Then in spring, the Italian mobilization for all-out war would be masked by the usual spring levies that collected recruits for the Roman army. All going well, in March 90 BC the Italian assault would come as a bolt from the blue and Rome would be on the ropes before the state even realized it was in danger. And if a sudden Italian attack immediately dropped

Rome into deep military trouble, then it would be politically easier for Italian diplomats to peel away Rome's allies by the same judicious mixture of bribes and threats that Rome usually used to keep them in line in the first place.

So the last thing the Italians wanted was to declare war late in the campaigning season. That would cost them the advantage of surprise without any benefit to compensate. If hostilities broke out right after the death of Drusus and late in the year, then the Italians would have at best a month in which to campaign before the harvest was safely behind Roman city walls and out of the reach of foragers. Thereafter the wet and soggy Italian autumn would make travel difficult for individuals, let alone for armies. Little could be achieved by the Italians in just one month, but if the war started in autumn, Rome would be forewarned and would then spend the winter shoring up vulnerable walls in the colonies and citadels, and shoring up shaky alliances in the surrounding countryside. It also meant that instead of expecting the Italians to turn up in their usual numbers for the spring levy, the Romans would desperately raise troops from their own citizenry from groups of the population usually left untapped. Altogether then, it was best that the Romans be left in ignorance of the nasty surprise awaiting them in the spring of 90 BC. And fortunately, that autumn circumstances had provided a typically Roman spat to distract the senate and people from matters outside the city.

The inadvertent cause of this spat was King Bocchus, the Mauretanian king who had ended the African war by handing Jugurtha over to Sulla (p.33). With everything that had gone on since, what with the Cimbric invasion and the uproar over Drusus' proposed reforms, Bocchus wanted to make sure that his contribution to expanding Rome's empire would not be forgotten. Therefore he proposed to set up a tableau in the Roman forum. Gilded statues would show the most dramatic event of the war, when king Bocchus loyally handed over the renegade king Jugurtha to the Romans. This would be a permanent reminder to the Romans of their diplomatic success and of the friendship of the Mauretanians. Who in Rome could object to that?

Actually Marius could. To his lasting chagrin, he had not been present at the hand-over. Therefore the Roman officer actually commemorated in the tableau would bestow glory on the wrong person – that is, on someone not called Caius Marius. At this point Marius already had rather a lot against

Sulla. Sulla already had a seal-ring depicting more or less the same scene that Bocchus was proposing to immortalize in stone, and that was annoying enough. But (when seen from a Marian perspective) Sulla had also had the insolence to have come out of the climactic battle against the Cimbri looking better than had Marius who, it will be recalled, had got lost while looking for the enemy and had only turned up when it was all over. Then, once the war was over, Marius' involvement in domestic politics had not been a success. He had allied himself with politicians of a demagogic inclination. This had proven to be a disaster, and though Marius had managed to stay alive while his populist colleagues had not, the same could not be said of his political career. The aristocratic senators had never been fond of Marius, and the politically powerful faction of the Metelli positively loathed him. With the senate currently in the ascendant, Marius was in danger of becoming a has-been.

> He had a house built for himself. It was near the forum because, he said, he didn't want those coming to him to pay their respects to have to walk a long way. Alternatively, he may have thought that distance was the reason why larger crowds flocked to the doors of others. However, the truth was somewhat different. He lacked both the skills of social interaction and the political ability to be useful. He was somewhat like an instrument of war in time of peace.
>
> Of all those who overshadowed him in popular esteem, none frustrated and angered him more than Sulla, who was rising to power ....
>
> Plutarch, *Life of Marius* 32

Therefore Bocchus' statues, which glorified Sulla and ignored Marius, threw oil on resentment already smouldering. Once he heard exactly what would be depicted in the proposed tableau, Marius mobilized his allies among the common people and demanded that the statues be taken down. The senate gleefully retorted that the statues were authorized, and the fact that they did not honour Marius was insufficient reason for their removal. The situation became rowdy 'and the city was all but in flames'[3] probably because Marius v. Sulla soon became a proxy fight for the people's continuing anger and resentment with the senate, which was channelled through Marius, and the senate sticking up for Sulla whom they considered one of their own.

However, instead of the situation in Rome taking people's minds off affairs in Italy as a whole, affairs in Italy instead ended up defusing the situation in Rome. This was due to the keen observation of an agent of one Servilius Caepio, of the clan of the Caepiones.[4] Caepio was one of the emissaries sent out by the senate to make sure that all in Italy remained calm after the murder of Drusus, and one of his sources had noted something unusual. A group of men had arrived in the city of Asculum, collected a youthful scion of the local nobility and taken him away. Asculum was in southern Picenum, Picenum being the area near the mouth of the river Po in North-eastern Italy described in Chapter 3. Picenum was largely occupied by Romans who had displaced the original inhabitants. Many of those displaced inhabitants had ended up living around Asculum, so suspicious activity among a dispossessed and bitter population merited close attention.

As it turned out that suspicion was warranted. What Caepio's spy had seen was a hostage being exchanged with another group of Italian conspirators as a guard against betrayal and defection. Caepio did not know this, but he knew that something untoward was happening, and he resolved to do something about it. The Caepiones have a long history in Rome, from the first consul in 253 BC all the way down to the Brutus Servilius Caepio who murdered Julius Caesar in 44 BC; and not a man of the entire clan was ever known for his tact and diplomacy. This particular specimen of the genus was no exception. Caepio proceeded to Asculum, and found the city in the middle of a festival. Given the issue of chronology discussed above, it is highly probable that this was a harvest festival, with merrymaking and the consumption of the previous year's vintage among the attractions. Into this celebration Caepio rudely intruded; forcing his way to a suitable vantage point from which he proceeded to harangue the crowd. According to Appian the general tone was threatening, but the exact context of his speech has not survived, because Caepio didn't either. His theme may have involved the power of the Roman armies, the perils of disobedience, and the fate of Fregellae (which had been flattened to the ground for disloyalty in the previous generation p.18). 'He talked to them not as allies and a free people, but as though they were slaves' notes the historian Diodorus Siculus.[5]

Such a speech was never going to go down well if delivered to a population moderately soused with wine, especially as that population had a deservedly bad conscience in any case. What result Caepio was expecting to get is unknown, but anyone without his familial pig-headedness could have expected what he got. The people of Asculum assumed that the game was up, and that Caepio knew about the intended rebellion. Since there was no point in dissembling any more, the townsfolk got right down to business and started the rebellion right there and then. Caepio was the first item on the agenda, and his subordinates were lynched alongside him. Then the people of Asculum turned on the Romans living in the city and killed them and looted their property. There was no keeping the secret after that, especially after word of the uprising reached other towns in the locality, which promptly followed the example of Asculum. As Italy trembled on the brink of war, the Italians sent a diplomatic mission to Rome in one last-ditch effort to make the senate see reason. It is possible that this was a tactical manoeuvre; that the hope of peace would keep Rome pacified until the planned assault could be launched in spring, but this is unlikely. Whatever happened, Rome was forewarned. It is more probable that the Italians genuinely and desperately wanted the Romans to let them have the citizenship without them having to fight a war to get it. If the Romans said 'no', then the planned war would go ahead. If, contrary to all precedent, the senate actually agreed to negotiate, then perhaps what the Italians wanted could be achieved without bloodshed. In any case, there was no harm in trying.

From the senate's point of view, their response was completely reasonable. If the Italians wanted to talk, the senate would consider their request. But not until full reparations had been made for the killings and destruction at Asculum, and not until after those who had perpetrated those crimes had paid for them. To the Italians this was not so much an opening position for negotiations as a flat refusal to negotiate at all. Peace had been a forlorn hope from the start, and even as the Italian delegates were demanding to be heard by the senate, Pompaedius Silo and his colleagues were hurrying around the towns and the countryside raising the banner of rebellion.

The first to take up arms were the Marsi, and they were always the most dangerous, for the Via Valeria ran past their lands to Corfinium – which city was now also in rebellion. A Marsic army on the smooth well-paved

Via Valeria was less than 100km (around 62 miles) from the centre of Rome itself. Probably the only thing that prevented the Marsi from making an immediate march on that largely unprepared city was the fact that the outbreak of the rebellion took the Marsi almost as much by surprise as the Romans. The Marsic leaders had assumed that the event was scheduled for the coming spring, and consequently their preparations were not yet complete. The Marsi were followed into rebellion by the Vestini, a Sabine tribe whom the Romans had forced into an alliance in 302 BC. The Sabines had always had close connections with Rome, as witnessed by the infamous Rape of the Sabines in the first years after the city's foundation, and many Romans were proud of their Sabine ancestry. However, inscriptions unearthed in Vestinian territory show that both in language and outlook, these particular Sabines had more in common with their Marsic neighbours than with Rome.

On the trans-Apennine side, another tribe of Marsic neighbours also pitched in. These were the Peligni. They were a mountain tribe occupying much of the region of Abruzzo in modern Italy. Most of the population occupied a high mountain valley, which was separated from the Marsi by the Fucine Lake (a body of water that was to prove of some military significance later) and a mountain ridge that provided the Peligni almost complete protection from invaders. The only breach of the mountain range was the deep gorge which took the Aternus River (the main river of the region) to the sea. And as the Aternus valley (the modern Gizio) led to the territory of the Peligni's fellow rebels, the Vestini, that route was also secure.

Closely related to the Peligni and the Vestini were the smaller tribe of the Marruncini. In fact both Vestini and Marruncini seem to have shared the port of Aternum (Pescara) on the west coast of central Italy. Just to the north of Aternum and the Vestini was Picentine territory. This meant that in west-central Italy a solid bloc of land was held by the rebels from just south of the mouth of the river Po through southern Picentine land, the territory of the Vestini and then of the Marruncini, finishing almost at the 'spur' above the heel of the boot of Italy. This took a large bite out of the territory over which Rome held sway, and with the addition of Marsic lands, that bite extended right across the peninsula to within reach of the city of Rome itself.

This initial wave of rebellion did much to ease the minds of those Italians considering rebellion, but afraid to share the fate of Fregellae, which had been brutally crushed for the want of allies. This time around, a second wave of rebels was not long in coming. No one had much doubted that the Samnites would be a part of that wave, and indeed they were. They would have been a part of the first wave, but for the fact that they were a rural people living in mountainous territory, and they had to cope with a number of large Roman colonies situated inconveniently across their lands. Like the Marsi, the Samnites were probably expecting a spring event, so it took them even longer to get an autumn rebellion properly organized. Once the Samnites went against Rome, their close relatives the Hirpini – whose lands surrounded the strategic Roman colony of Beneventum – joined in the rebellion; and the nearby Lucanians (p.00) promptly followed their lead. The tide of rebellion continued to sweep across southern Italy, and Apulia now also declared against Rome. With the addition of the tribe of the Frentani, who occupied the coast north-west of the Samnites, almost the entire Adriatic seaboard of Italy apart from Roman Picenum had joined the Italian revolt.[6]

The west and south were soon joined by parts of the south-east, as represented by the city of Pompeii. The nearby city of Acerrae stayed loyal, and was to be an important Roman military base in the years that followed. It was far from co-incidental that the people of Pompeii had been denied the citizenship, while Acerrae was the first city to have been made a Roman *civitas sine suffragio* in 332 BC, and the initially hostile citizens there had by now been Romans for two centuries. The rebellion in the east was not unanimous. Even though Umbria and Etruria trembled on the brink, they eventually pulled back from declaring war, though the question of whether to do so was fiercely debated up and down the towns and cities of both regions. Nor was everyone in rebel territory a rebel. In Campania, the native people raised a militia to support the Romans. In Lucania the Roman emissary Servius Galba (an ancestor of the later emperor of AD 69) had apparently mistaken the friendliness of the lady with whom he was lodging for the friendliness of the people whose mood he was sent to ascertain. He was caught by the sudden rebellion, but was freed from captivity by the good offices of his former hostess.[7] In fact it is clear that in many cases, especially in Apulia, influential aristocrats managed to keep their particular communities loyal to Rome even as the rest of the countryside rose in rebellion.

At this point of absolute and vital importance was the attitude of the Latins and the colonists. The 'Latins' were those people who possessed the Latin Right, the right to make commercial agreements, to marry or transfer citizenship to another Latin state if they moved there. This right gave Latins many of the privileges of Roman citizenship. Though Latins did not have the vote, they were protected by Roman law and were thus safe from the worst of the abuses that had been inflicted on the Italians. The colonies, those fortified outposts scattered around the hostile lands of the south and west of Italy, were designed precisely to hold those lands under Roman control. However, the populations of these colonies had large numbers of *peregrini* – foreigners living within the city walls. And many of the 'Romans' in these colonies had never even seen Rome but were closely linked to neighbouring Italian cities through marriage, commerce and culture. So whether the Latins would stay loyal was already an open question, but it was a particularly moot question in the case of those colonies with a population of Latins, and these colonies tended to be much larger than purely Roman settlements.

A good example of such a colony was Venusia, in Apulia. This town was allegedly founded by Diomedes, a Greek hero from the Trojan war. It had been a Latin colony since its capture by Rome in 262 BC, and the city had stood steadfastly with Rome throughout the Hannibalic war. It had done so even though that war had so devastated the city that afterwards Rome had sent 20,000 citizens to repopulate the place, despite the Romans being somewhat short of manpower themselves at the time. However, in recent years Venusia had developed a strong Apulian accent, as people from the countryside flocked in to share the city's growing prosperity. Now the loyalty of the population was about to be severely tested. When war broke out no one doubted that the colonies were going to be attacked. They occupied some of the richest land in southern Italy and had been located at choke points in overland communications with the express purpose of being a crippling nuisance to any rebels. Whether the colonists were prepared to withstand the privations of siege from people with whom they shared so many bonds, and whether they would be prepared to kill and be killed in defence of a deeply flawed and unjust Roman state that had done little to merit such service was a question that would ultimately decide the future of Italy. The Venusians deliberated these questions and found Rome wanting. They threw in their lot with the rebels, and the whole peninsula held its breath while waiting to discover how many other colonies were going to join them.

As it turned out, the defection of the Latins and the colonies started and stopped at Venusia. Had it not, Rome would not have survived. The military significance of the colonies goes without saying. The military significance of the other Latin tribes is less remarked upon, but they were the weight that finally tipped the scales. Every tribe and region that rebelled counted as double in this coming war, because apart from the somewhat bemused Gallic regions of northern Italy, there were few neutrals. You either fought for Rome, or you fought against it. So every city that went over to the rebels deprived the Romans of the soldiers that Rome would otherwise be able to levy. Instead the rebels supplied those same soldiers to the Italian side. So, if for example, the Romans lost the loyalty of 30,000 Latin soldiers and the Italians gained these men, then the difference between the Italian army and the Roman army became 60,000 men. Given that each side came into the conflict with about 100,000 men under arms, that 60,000 made a crucial difference.

Another question weighed on the minds of Romans of a thoughtful disposition – what about the rest of the empire, and of the lands beyond? Rome at this time had a substantial but untidy empire stretching from eastern Spain to beyond the eastern shores of the Aegean Sea. What happened if the peoples of these lands took it in their heads to rebel, or even worse, to make common cause with the Italians? This last possibility at least was vanishingly remote. Whatever their differences at home, Italians and Romans abroad had co-operated enthusiastically in exploiting the lands they had jointly conquered. Indeed, this exploitation at times approached the point of pillage, and the resentful peoples being plundered cared little about the political disagreements of their hated occupiers. The idea that they might side with one against the other lost its attraction to foreigners when both sets of oppressors appeared equally unsavoury.

Rebellion against both Romans and Italians was a different matter, but here the Romans' best defence was the conquered peoples themselves. Generally speaking, the Spaniards and Greeks did not think of themselves in nationalist terms as such, but as, for example, Celtiberians, Vascones, Athenians and Beotians. Local rivalries tended to trump anti-Roman feeling, so if the Celtiberians were to rebel (and they did eventually), then it was a sure bet that the Vascones would immediately take the Roman side (as they did). Likewise, the Athenians and Beotians did not declare for the Italian side because if one did so, the other would immediately become patriotically Roman.

This left invaders from outside the empire. Fortunately candidates for this role were few, since in the decades leading up to their civil war Rome and the Italians had done an effective job of beating up any potential foreign threats. Gaul was too disorganized to mount an invasion, and there currently were no large tribal movements that might cause one. Though independent, Egypt was politically a mess and lacked the will and the means to intervene in Roman affairs. Parthia was at this time a remote country with little interest in Roman affairs. Indeed, the two empires had not yet even properly introduced themselves through a formal meeting of ambassadors, though this was about to happen.

That left Pontus. Pontus was one of those kingdoms that had arisen in Asia Minor after the Roman-induced decline of the Seleucid empire. Pontus was very wealthy, probably because the political and military chaos of the failing Seleucid empire to the south had diverted the end point of the fabled Silk Road through the stable and well-ruled kingdom. The current king was Mithridates VI, a man of considerable political ability and intellectual capacity. Mithridates was also cruel, ambitious and expansionist. He had already extended his rule into Armenia minor and the kingdoms on the northern shore of the Black Sea, and was hungrily eyeing the neighbouring kingdoms of Cappadocia and Bithynia in Asia Minor. In fact, even as war broke out in Italy, ambassadors were en route to Pontus to demand that Mithridates hand back control of both kingdoms. Mithridates had engineered a palace coup in Bithynia and an Armenian invasion of Cappadocia and set up client kings subservient to him in both places. Rome had a long history of trying to keep Mithridates in check, and did so not by sweet reason but with the threat of the Roman legions. What Mithridates would do once he heard that those legions were about to start tearing each other apart in Italy was too painful to contemplate.

So as Rome began urgently to prepare for war in Italy, the senate did so with nervous glances eastward. News arrived at the Capitol that the Italians had appointed generals and established their own capital in the central Apennine city of Confinium at the other end of the via Valeria. This city was now renamed Italica to show the unity of the rebels, who now laid siege to the Roman colonies of Alba and Aesernia. By mid-autumn 91 BC, the peace had irrevocably broken down. Diplomacy and negotiation had failed; it was time to give war a chance.

Chapter 6

90 BC – Backs to the Wall

From the manner of its response to the crisis, we learn much about the state of mind of the Roman senate. Rome was faced with a threat potentially more dangerous than that of Hannibal in 216 BC. Hannibal had managed to conquer much of southern Italy – now much of southern Italy had voluntarily turned against Rome. Hannibal might have been a military genius, but without that genius his rag-tag army of Gauls and Spaniards were no match for the more numerous, better-armed and disciplined Roman legions. This time around, the Romans faced an enemy as numerous as they were, who were every bit as much disciplined and ferocious fighters, and who knew the Roman military system intimately. While it was true that there was no Hannibal in the Italian ranks, all the Roman senate had to offer for leadership of their own armies were the same petty-minded and self-interested individuals who had brought about the disaster in the first place. This was proven by the fact that, with the city facing extinction, the immediate reaction of the political class was to use the crisis for infighting and to settle scores with personal enemies.

Taking advantage of popular disquiet at the Italian uprising, the tribune-elect Quintus Varius Hybrida proposed a law called the *lex Varia de maiestate*. *Maiestas* already existed as an offence in the Roman statute books. It was the crime of 'diminishing the majesty of the Roman people'. This was a sort of catch-all law designed to punish those shenanigans of morally lax senators for which no specific legal statute had been designed. *Maiestas* covered issues such as forging public documents, ordering the release of prisoners justly confined, occupying public spaces and showing undue favour to Rome's enemies for whatever reason. However the activities punishable by *maiestas* legislation were poorly specified, precisely because of the law's catch-all nature. Basically *maiestas* was whatever a court and jury decided it was in the case of a particular individual. With a political system as cynically corrupt as that in Rome the potential for abuse of such laws was vast.

Varius' take on *maiestas* was that aspects of the law should be refined to punish those who had shown sympathy to the Italian rebels. Of course, no such sympathy need be expressed on the public record, nor need the charges be particularly plausible. The court's main purpose was to dispose of the rivals and enemies of the faction backing Q. Varius; and the Italian revolt had given that faction its excuse. The historian Appian explicitly says as much, accusing the equites of backing Varius and 'hoping to bring all the senators under this shameful indictment, and themselves to sit in judgement on them'.[1] Later historians have looked at other factions, including that party in the senate most opposed to Livius Drusus and now eager for revenge on his associates.

As the near-contemporary legal commentator Asconius remarked, the court quickly gained a name for unjust condemnations.[2] Lucius Memmius, an ally of Drusus, was quickly condemned and he was followed by such distinguished names as Aurelius Cotta (a relative of Julius Caesar in the maternal line). Calpurnius Bestia was probably prosecuted, this being a populist measure against the general who had disreputably enriched himself by taking bribes to go easy on Jugurtha in the African war of 112 BC, and who was widely seen as having got away with it. However, in looking for popular esteem by punishing past sinners Varius decided to go for bigger game still. If he could get Bestia, why not that old rogue Aemilius Scaurus who had not only avoided bribery charges, but had been appointed to lead the investigation into those charges? Scaurus was a dangerous foe. As a member of Rome's great Aemilian family he had the power and prestige that came with the name, and he had built upon that to create a nexus of political friends and connections unequalled in Rome at that time. The actual trial was brief. Here is how Scaurus presented his case:

Quintus Caepio hoped that he had found the chance to destroy his old enemy Scaurus. He persuaded the tribune Q. Varius [Hybrida] to summon the seventy-two year old Scaurus to face charges. ... Scaurus appeared, supported on the arms of young men of the highest nobility. In reply to the charges, he had this to say 'The Spaniard Q. Varius alleges that Marcus Aemilius Scaurus, leader of the senate, has incited treachery in our allies. Marcus Aemilius Scaurus, leader of the senate, denies the charges. Citizens of the jury, whom do you choose to believe?'

Asconius commentary on *pro Scauro* 22C

Varius' cognomen of 'Hybrida' was the source of Scaurus' 'Spaniard' appellation. A 'hybridus' was a person of joint Roman-Spanish parentage, and Scaurus used the name to point out that the man accusing Romans of consorting with foreigners had himself been born of a foreign mother. It was a low blow, but it worked. Scaurus was acquitted by popular acclamation. That is, so enthusiastically did the audience applaud the defendant that Varius decided it was wisest to drop charges on the spot. It did not help him. The following year, when he was no longer protected by his tribunican office, Varius found himself hauled before the very court he had established and was found guilty. He died soon afterwards in mysterious circumstances, though a conscientious coroner would have put 'giving mortal offence to a powerful Roman' on the death certificate.

Meanwhile the war went on, and it had started badly for Rome. The main features of the highly curtailed autumn campaign of 91 were the Italian sieges of Aesernia in Samnite territory and Alba Fucensis, the latter as its name implies, being on the via Valeria near the Fucine lake. Both were well-defended cities on steep hills, Aesernia on a crag rising over 300 metres between two rivers in the Volturnus valley, and Alba on one of the steep foothills before Mons Velinus. Both garrisons had capable commanders, and no one expected an immediate resolution to either siege. Otherwise military action was minimal. Apart from preoccupations with political back-biting in Rome, the two sides were mainly engaged in preparing for the main confrontation in the coming year.

The Italians had followed the Roman pattern of taking two 'consuls', though these were consuls in the old Roman sense by which a consul was primarily a war leader. Naturally one of those commanders was the leader and instigator of the entire rebellion, Pompaedius Silo. The other consul, Papius Mutilus, represented the Samnites, who along with Silo's Marsi made up the two most important rebel groups. Silo commanded the 'northern' group – that is, the least southerly group of rebels that operated close to

Rome – and Mutilus took the southern group of tribes. This was a very rough and ready division, but it is probable that each group focussed on one siege, with a general from the 'southern' group taking command of the siege of Aesernia in the south, and one of Silo's commanders doing the same for Alba.[3] The division of command also reflected the linguistic division of the two groups. As their coinage shows, the northern group used Latin as their lingua franca while the southerners spoke Oscan, and they called Mutilus, their commander, *embratur* – a word that may well be the original of the Latin '*imperator*' from which we today get 'emperor'.

The Romans meanwhile chose their generals with particular care. As consul for the coming year they elected one of the Julii Caesares, an ancient family newly come again into political prominence. Lucius Julius Caesar was to take command of the war against the southern group of rebels and his colleague Rutilius Lupus would handle the Marsi and others close to Rome. This Rutilius was a relative of that Rutilius Rufus still in comfortable exile in Asia Minor and watching all the excitement from afar. Unsurprisingly the feuding but very competent Sulla and Marius were separated under the command of different consuls. Caesar didn't get Marius, which is surprising as the pair were close family through Marius' marriage to a Julian wife. However Rutilius Lupus was also a relative, and once he had got Marius in the north, Caesar perforce got Sulla in the south.

In selecting their generals, the Romans were more concerned with military proficiency than politics. This led to some odd combinations. Also under Caesar's command was Titus Didius, the man who had authored the *lex Caecilia Didia*, which had been used to demolish Drusus' legislation in 91 BC. Yet so too was Licinius Crassus, a relative of that Crassus who had supported Drusus in the senate. Likewise Rutilius' generals included not only the populist Marius, but that Caepio who had been at the forefront of those opposing the populist measures of Drusus. Another of Rutilius' generals worthy of note was Gnaeus Pompeius Strabo, a cynical opportunist best known to posterity for fathering a son also called Gnaeus Pompeius, who is better known to us today as Pompey the Great. 'These were men who had learned the art of war, not from books but from action and victory in the field' remarks Cicero,[4] and he should know, since at this time Cicero was enrolled as a young junior officer on the staff of the aforesaid Pompeius Strabo.

The troops that Italians and Romans commanded were very much alike. Both sides relied on heavy infantry to win their battles, and it is probable that both used the cohort formations that had become the standard unit of their armies since Marius had employed them so effectively against the Cimbri. Some of the Samnites may have adopted their traditional armour of stiffened linen, but generally most of those called to arms on either side would have donned the same coats of chain mail that they would have worn had they served together in Rome's foreign wars that year. Each set of infantry relied on a heavy throwing spear (*pilum*) to be used just before engaging in hand-to-hand combat with a sword. A surviving fragment of the work of Roman historian Cassius Dio tells us how similar the two sides were. The Marsi were able to spy on the Romans 'by mingling with their forage parties and entering through their ramparts under the guise of allies. There they took note of what was seen and heard in the [Roman] camp and later reported this to their own side.'[5] In other words, even when the two sides were at war, it was hard to tell them apart.

As a general rule, the Italians had more skirmishers, since the hillmen from allied tribes were accustomed to this sort of fighting, and as a bonus many were also expert with the sling. On the other hand, the Romans had the better cavalry, both because they could recruit warriors skilled in this arm of combat from Cisalpine Gaul, and because most of northern Campania had stayed loyal and this region traditionally provided the Roman army with the bulk of its cavalry. Nevertheless, with both sides so equally matched in weapons, skill and numbers, the war would be decided by whichever side had the generals better able to outmanoeuvre their opponents, and which group had the politicians better able to maintain their own alliances and pick apart those of the other side. Given the wealth of military experience among the Roman generals, and the colossal ineptitude of their politicians (who were often the same people), one might expect victories in the field to be cancelled out by political setbacks. In fact the reverse was the case. In the year 90 BC, it was Rome's generals who brought the state to the brink of collapse, and the politicians who pulled them away from it.

The exact chronology of the war is lost to us for two reasons. One is that Rome's historians had little taste for telling stories of Roman defeats, and these were the main stories of 90 BC. The other is that most of Rome's historians of this period are as lost as were the battles they would otherwise be describing. Livy's superb and detailed history survives only as a brutally edited synopsis, and the usually reliably back-up, Cassius Dio, survives as a few fragments. Modern researchers can complain most bitterly about the near-total loss of the *Historiae* of Sisenna, a contemporary historian who wrote so detailed an account of the war that others, including Sallust, felt there was little to add and so left the topic alone. So we are left with the somewhat arbitrary and unreliable duo of Velleius Paterculus and Appian, both of whom rush through the events of 90 BC as a prologue to the later events of that century. To this scanty reserve of information we can add firstly the incidental comments of those present at the time, such as Cicero, and secondly the biographer Plutarch who wrote of the lives of both Sulla and Marius and also wrote the biographies of others who witnessed the events of the war as children or young men, including Cicero, Pompey, Crassus and Julius Caesar. Consequently, while a detailed narrative cannot be recounted, an outline of the year can be reconstructed, and from the Roman viewpoint it is not a pretty tale.

In the spring of 90 BC the little city of Pinna in the territory of the Sabine Vestini was one of the many communities that was violently divided as to which side to support. While the rest of the district was swayed by the neighbouring Marsi into declaring for the rebels, Pinna came down on the Roman side, albeit after a prolonged period of civil strife. As with Alba Fucensis, the city came under immediate siege by the rebels, and like Alba Fucensis, the city defended itself spiritedly. Little is known about the opening campaigns of the year, though the strategic aims of both sides are reasonably clear. For the Marsi and their allies, the immediate priority was to break the ring of Roman colonies that dominated the strategic landscape. The existence of these colonies meant that the Italians had to be constantly on the alert lest the Romans sally out from their walls and attack Marsic towns, farms and supply chains. But even more annoyingly, the colonies had been situated with malice aforethought across the major lines of communication in central Italy. This meant that Roman armies could zip about with relative ease, getting supplies and a safe haven each time they stopped at a colony. The Italians on the other hand had to laboriously get around each of these municipal roadblocks either by extensive detours or by struggling through difficult terrain. Militarily the Italians could not operate freely until the colonies had been taken out of the war so the colonies had to go for that reason alone, but there was also a political aspect, in that the colonies represented Roman domination of the people and the lands around. If the Italians were fighting to be rid of Roman domination then the colonies – the aspect of Rome which most impinged on their daily lives – would have to go too.

For the southern rebels too the Roman colonies were a huge inconvenience. However, the tactic of the Samnite commander Papius Mutilus was somewhat different. While the Marsi concentrated on breaking the ring of colonies that surrounded them, the southern group aimed at consolidating and extending the territory under their control by taking the countryside and smaller towns away from Rome. The example of Venusia had shown that opinion in the southern colonies was not unanimously pro-Roman. The further from Rome it was, the more likely it was that the population had 'gone native' as the Venusians had done. Therefore colonies in the south of Italy, cut off from Rome and with the Italians in control of the countryside, might decide to re-think their loyalties. Furthermore, not everyone in a colony had to join the rebel side. With a bit of luck and a lot of treachery, all it might take was a few dozen men prepared to open a critical gate at the right time. So Mutilus' operations had the focus of beating the Romans in the field, but not simply because from the Italian point of view this was a good thing in itself. Victory also helped to sway the hearts and minds of waverers, and where sympathy for the rebels was not enough, Mutilus was happy to add a healthy dose of terror by demonstrating the consequences of resistance.

The Roman strategy on the other hand could be summarized with the words defend, consolidate, survive. That is, the Romans had to defend their colonies for exactly the same reasons as the Italians needed to take them out of the war. This meant making sure that the colonies were strong enough in materiel and morale to withstand assault. An important aspect of morale for colonies that might come under siege was the probability of relief, so for the Romans preventing the fall of those places already under siege was a priority. As well as defending their colonies, the Romans had to consolidate the areas they currently held. This involved keeping a close eye on those Etrurians and Umbrians who were sympathetic to the rebel cause, and taking direct action against those areas such as Asculum which were already in revolt. Above all, Rome had to keep a grip on Campania. This area was horribly exposed to the rebels, with the Marsi to the north-east, the Samnites to the east and rebel Pompeii right on the doorstep. Yet without Campania Rome had few resources in Italy with which to fight the war. As Cicero later remarked, 'don't forget the powerful armies we maintained on the Campanian harvests when all other sources of revenue had been lost'.[6]

With the heartlands secured, it would thereafter be a war in which the Romans attempted to grind down the Italians in much the same way as the Romans had ground down Hannibal a century previously. The trick was not so much to win victories as to avoid defeat. Rome had an empire and could draw on it for money and manpower and if necessary simply outlast the Italians. This technique had worked with Hannibal, and it would work on the Italians, since after all the Italians that Rome was now fighting were pretty much the same Italians who had allied with Hannibal in that previous conflict. However, in order to wear down the Italians in the long term, Rome had to survive for the short term – and that was to prove none too easy.

The campaigning season kicked off with an early and obscure engagement between the armies of one of Rutilius' subordinates, a commander called Gaius Perpenna, and an Italian general called Presentius. Since Perpenna was under Rutilius' command we can assume that, like Rutilius, Perpenna was engaged in fighting the Marsi and their allies. Therefore Perpenna's engagement must have taken place in central Italy, but exactly where is unknown. Whatever happened to Perpenna's army was certainly a defeat, for it resulted in 4,000 Romans dead and many others captured. Evidently Perpenna's handling of the army was at fault, because Rutilius relieved Perpenna of his command and transferred the remnant of his army to Marius. Marius and his men were then merged into a larger army, which Rutilius intended to lead against the Marsi. Meanwhile things were not going well on the southern front either. In Lucania, Caesar's subordinate, Licinius Crassus, took a beating. From a reference in an unrelated text[7] we find that Crassus pitched camp in dry woodland. The Italians under a general called Marcus Lamponius set fire to the woods, and in the subsequent confusion killed some 800 of Crassus' men. Thereafter Crassus and his forces narrowly escaped being trapped by the Italian forces thrusting into Campania and had to take refuge in Hannibal's old headquarters, the town of Grumentum (near Grumento Nova in the modern province of Potenza).[8]

Marius' brother-in-law was Sextus Julius Caesar, a relative and subordinate of the Lucius Julius Caesar who was currently consul. Sextus'[9] attempt to head off reinforcements to the Italians besieging Aesernia came to a sorry end with the loss of 2,000 men. This left Aesernia with major problems. Like the rest of Italy, Aesernia had not been expecting hostilities to break out in 91 BC so the city had little in the way of provisions with which to withstand a siege. Starvation had become a serious problem. Had Sextus Julius Caesar managed to defeat the Italian reinforcements he might have had a chance of relieving the siege in conjunction with a sally from those Romans penned within Aesernia's walls. As it was, having seen off Sextus Julius Caesar the Italian reinforcements made direct for Aesernia. Once the extra Italians arrived, the city was doomed. Sulla was operating in the area and did the best he could against the more numerous enemy, which gave the Aesernians hope. Consequently, the garrison held out as long as it could, but hunger eventually opened the gates. It was some consolation to Rome that the Italians failed to capture the two men who had led the defence of the city. These men – Lucius Scipio and Lucius Acilius – disguised themselves as slaves and slipped away undetected.

Aesernia was far from the only town which the Romans lost in the opening months of the war. Once Aesernia had fallen the way lay open to Venafrum in Campania at the mid-point between Latium and Samnite territory. It was taken through treachery by the Samnite Marius Egnatius (who was possibly a descendant of the Marius Egnatius who had inflicted telling defeats on the Romans in the wars of the third century BC). Meanwhile, the Samnite 'consul' Papius Mutilus was sweeping through the towns and countryside further south around Pompeii.

The Romans hoped that Mutilus could be stopped at Nola, a city strategically situated between the Apennines and Mt Vesuvius. Hannibal had so much trouble with this city that no fewer than three battles were fought outside its walls during the Hannibalic war. However, Mutilus had laid his plans well, and he had arranged that the city would be betrayed to him as his army approached. Along with Nola, Mutilus captured the city's garrison of 2,000 men. These men were offered the opportunity of changing to the winning (Italian) side, and gratefully took it. Their officers, including the praetor Lucius Postumus, refused to abandon the Roman cause and were subsequently starved to death as a demonstration that Mutilus refused to tolerate resistance.

Mutilus used terror as a tactical weapon. When he took a town, the leading Roman citizens were executed, and presumably any who sympathized too openly with them. Mutilus so viciously plundered the countryside that Appian says 'the towns in the vicinity were terrified and surrendered to him'.[10] In quick order Stabiae and Herculaneum on the coast, the nearby Roman colony of Salernum and several other towns fell to the Italian leader, who forcibly recruited the available manpower into his army, thus gaining about two legions and a thousand cavalry. Next Mutilus headed for Acerrae, a town situated inland some thirteen miles from Naples. The consul Lucius Caesar now entered the fray. Thanks to the energetic recruiting of an up-and-coming officer in Cisalpine Gaul, Caesar had acquired reinforcements of ten thousand Gallic warriors. Recruitment elsewhere in the empire had added a formidable force of Numidian horse, cavalry generally reckoned the best light horse in the world. But Mutilus had also foreseen the arrival of the Numidians and had taken steps to neutralize them.

It will be remembered that the Latin colony of Venusia in Apulia had defected early to the Italian side. In Venusia the Romans had been holding hostage one of the sons of Jugurtha, and this man had fallen into Mutilus' hands along with the city. Now this scion of the Numidian royal line was displayed to his father's former subjects. The Numidians were invited to desert Rome and fight for a member of their own royal family. So many took that invitation that Caesar was forced to consider the rest of his Numidian cavalry untrustworthy and he therefore sent them back to Africa.

Things had been going so well for Mutilus that he might be excused for getting a little cocky. He now decided that his own men were still buoyed by their victories around Aesernia while the Numidian defection must have lowered Roman morale even further. The Samnite leader therefore decided to make a direct assault on Caesar's camp. Attacking a Roman marching camp was a risky venture because the Romans had a lot of practice both at building and defending these camps. However, if the attack was successful, not only would it take a large proportion of the Roman army out of the war, but losing thousands of their men might make the Cisalpine Gauls considerably less eager to supply the Roman army with recruits in the future. The Italians attacked ferociously and made a breach on the palisade on one side of Caesar's camp.

Their understandable concentration on enlarging and forcing their way through this breach led to the Italians' undoing, because no one was watching the other gates. (A Roman camp usually had four.) Lucius Caesar had not lost all his cavalry. Apart from native Campanians, a substantial Mauretanian contingent had arrived along with the Numidians, and the Mauretanians and their king Bocchus were enthusiastically pro-Roman. So Lucius Caesar and his cavalry made their way out of one of the unguarded gates and swept down on the flanks and rear of the Italian attackers. The result was the first substantial Italian defeat of the war. The camp was saved and some 6,000 Italians were killed. This was news so cheering that when it reached Rome the senate decreed that the population should resume wearing the togas they had stopped wearing as a sign that their country was struggling at war. Less encouragingly, Caesar took a hard look at the forces arrayed against him at Acerrae and decided that he lacked the strength to oppose them. He withdrew, leaving Acerrae to stand siege by Mutilus and his Italians.

At the same time news arrived that the town of Canusium had fallen to the rebels, which meant that Brundisium was the only substantial town in the area still in Roman hands, and Brundisium was now isolated. Nor was this merely the isolation of a single city, for Brundisium was the port which served as Rome's access to Greece and Asia. With communication to Brundisium cut off, access to the eastern empire had suddenly become much more difficult. Nor were things going well in the rest of eastern Italy. Pompeius Strabo had been given the job of bringing Asculum to heel. This was an obvious choice, for Strabo was a major landowner in the more romanized part of Picenum to the north. He knew both the terrain and the people, and he had plenty to lose, for while the rebels held Asculum they had a springboard to attack his own lands in Picenum. In fact Asculum was at a nexus of road communications. From Asculum not only Picenum but also Umbria and Cisalpine Gaul were highly accessible to the rebels. Apart from Asculum's strategic value, there were other reasons for wanting the town captured as soon as possible, namely the political and propaganda prize that the Romans would gain if they captured the town and avenged the massacre of Roman citizens there when the revolt had first flared up.

However, disappointment awaited any Romans who hoped that Asculum would prove to be the one bright spot in a year of military setbacks. Pompeius Strabo was no mean general, but the odds were stacked against him. For a start, the opposing commanders, particularly one Vettius Scato, were pretty good at generalship themselves. Vettius Scato was a lively commander and it was he (or a relative) who had prevented Caesar from being able to lift the siege of Aesernia on the southern front. In Picenum, Scato had a strong force of Marsi eager to prove that their ferocious reputation was justified. The people of Asculum were themselves a warlike bunch, and they had a generation-old grudge against the Romans for taking their lands to the north. Furthermore, Asculum itself was a hard nut to crack. It sat on a large rocky ledge where the modern Tronto river is joined to the river Castellano. In fact the city had waterways on three sides and a steep hill on the other. There is also a suggestion in Orosius that Asculum had a loose alliance with pirates who helped with supplies – something not completely improbable although the city was far enough from the coast for direct supply to be impracticable. A fragment of Cassius Dio[11] suggests that immediately after their uprising the people of Asculum went onto the offensive: 'They overcame those who had not yet joined the rebellion … and tore the skin off the heads of their wives along with the hair.'

Pompeius Strabo's charge to the rescue was not a success. He was halted in his tracks by the Marsi, and forced to retreat northwards to the mountains. The rebels followed up, and forced Pompeius Strabo and his battered army to take refuge in the town of Firmum on the Adriatic coast. So Pompeius Strabo ended up some 40 kilometres north-east of the city he was meant to assault, and instead of restoring Rome's tattered military glory, the would-be conqueror of Asculum had added Firmum to the list of pro-Roman cities under Italian siege.

Vettius Scato did not stay to press the siege. Leaving this in the hands of a subordinate he headed back into central Italy, where Rutilius Lupus was about to make his big push into Marsic territory. After the action with Perpenna, the war in central Italy had been little more than skirmishing along the via Valeria. This was about to be replaced with serious action, because Rutilius Lupus wanted to strike a telling blow against the Marsi. Not only were these people the elite forces on the Italian side, but they were the enemy group closest to Rome. Also, Rutilius now had Perpenna's setback to avenge. Accordingly, he marched out against the Marsic enemy with an army of undisclosed size, but which we can roughly estimate as being four legions, or (because legions were generally below their theoretical strength of 6,000) at a very rough guess, 20,000 men.

As his second-in-command Rutilius had Marius. Even if he had done so before, it is doubtful that Rutilius still considered it a blessing to have Marius as a subordinate. As anyone who knew Marius might have supposed, the six-times consul did not work well under another's command. As Marius no doubt frequently informed his commanding officer, he was by far the more experienced general, and was free with his advice. Marius was also by nature a very cautious campaigner, and the fact that he was personally in command of men who had recently suffered a morale-breaking defeat made him yet more so. 'Marius was constantly suggesting in private that a delay would prove beneficial to the conduct of the war and that the young recruits ought to be drilled in camp' the writer Orosius tells us.[12] A slow approach was in any case Marius' preferred form of combat; to delay battle, keep close to the enemy, wait for a mistake and then force an action on favourable ground. In the meantime, skirmishing and minor clashes would harden the nerves of the men and accustom them to the enemy and their tactics. With the Marian method, the foe seemed familiar and less terrifying when the crunch came, and success was more likely.

Rutilius was more of a traditionalist, and the traditional approach of a Roman general was to march his men to the battlefront, point them at the enemy army and thereafter encourage them to victory through the ensuing carnage. Besides tradition, there was another reason for the bull-at-a-gate strategy. Alba Fucensis remained under siege. Like Aesernia the citadel town had not been expecting a war in 91 BC, and had no reason to have laid in supplies for one. If this strategic location was not relieved in the near future then it would probably fall to the Marsi. Therefore Rutilius did not intend to be subtle about breaking the siege. He advanced directly to the River Tolenus, probably arriving at a point just north of the Via Valeria, near the city of Carsoli and less than 50 kilometres (30 miles) from Alba. Here the Monte Bove pass is created by the river as it flows down from the mountains making this one of the two natural approaches into Marsic territory from Latium. Naturally, the Marsi in their turn prepared to head the Romans off at the pass. The crossing of the river was contested by the Marsic army under the command of Vettius Scato who, as mentioned above, had returned from Picenum to take charge.

Perhaps surprisingly, Rutilius chose to divide his army, keeping half under his own command and giving Marius a free hand with his own unit. The two parts of the army separated and each began to attempt to force a crossing at a different point of the river. This manoeuvre was presumably to force Scato to divide his own forces accordingly, since he otherwise would have to concede the crossing to whichever army he was not facing. However, there is also a sneaking suspicion that for Rutilius the act of dividing his forces had the added advantage of getting Marius out of his face for at least a while. At first it looked as though Scato planned to sit on the fence, for he positioned his army between the two Roman forces. This was sensible enough, since if the Roman crossing was not perfectly co-ordinated, Scato could defeat the Romans in detail by moving against whomever crossed first, and then coming back to deal with the remaining Roman force, and all the while having the advantage of numbers. Eventually though, Scato appeared to change his mind, and shifted his army to oppose the crossing of Marius, leaving Rutilius to cross unopposed upstream. However, this was only an appearance. In fact the troops facing Marius were a thinly manned screen, for Scato knew his opponent. The cautious Marius would only advance once he had ascertained that Scato was bluffing, and it would take hours of careful probing and reconnaissance before Marius was sure that the enemy had too few men to prevent him from reaching the other side of the river.

The majority of the Marsic army was gone. The soldiers had withdrawn during the night, and were now waiting in ambush in crevasses and ravines near the newly completed bridge of Rutilius. Scato knew that Rutilius was much more likely to advance without cautious reconnaissance, being both eager to relieve Alba and deceived into believing that the bulk of the enemy army was downstream watching Marius. And so it proved. On the fateful morning of 11 June, Rutilius led his men across the river and straight into the carefully laid trap. The Romans were expecting minimal resistance, and instead they got almost the entire Marsic army.

We can assume that the Marsi fell on their victims before the Romans had properly organized to move inland, for they were quickly driven back on to the river. Scato had waited until the Romans were all across, because once the ambush was sprung, there was no way that such a large body of men could manage an orderly retreat across one makeshift bridge. Instead they were caught between the Marsi and the River Tolenus with neither time to organize a defence nor anywhere to run. Casualties were horrendous. It did not help the co-ordination of the Roman defence that the commander Rutilius was hit in the head by a missile and died in action, while the second-in-command, Marius was elsewhere and at this point unaware that there was even a battle taking place. According to the poet Ovid – writing several decades later with perfect hindsight – the death of Rutilius had been foretold by the Roman Goddess, the Magna Matua (the great mother).

> They say she asked you, Rutilius, 'Where are you rushing?
> As consul you'll fall to the Marsian enemy on my day.'[13]
> Her words were fulfilled, the Tolenus
> Flowed purple, its waters mixed with blood.
>
> Ovid *Fasti* 6.555

It was in fact this purple flow, and the bodies that came floating down along the river that alerted Marius that matters upstream were not going well. (It is these same bodies that let later historians know that the Romans were pushed back against the river.) The number of corpses made it clear to Marius that the majority of Scato's army was committed upstream against the other Roman force. Therefore by simple deduction, the force facing Marius had to be merely a flimsy screen, which could be smashed through with ease. Once Marius had done the math he acted with the speed and energy he always displayed when he knew the enemy were at a disadvantage. He swiftly crossed the river and after ascertaining the whereabouts of Scato's camp, he captured that while the Marsic leader was engaged with the stubborn remnants of Rutilius Lupus' force.

If we are to believe Orosius, a writer who described events from a perspective of four centuries afterwards, Marius then swiftly counter-attacked. If he did so, and caught the Marsi unprepared then the body-count of 8,000 Marsi dead in the battle is quite credible. What is less credible is that the much earlier historian Appian, writing in about AD 155, does not mention this most dramatic Roman victory of the war to date, and his is the best continuous history of the war still extant. However, whether the Marsi suffered a defeat or merely a minor setback, in either case Scato had to withdraw. We know from another of those informative fragments of Dio that the Romans were the better-supplied of the two armies, and the loss of the Marsic camp and the rations stored within could not have helped Scato's logistical situation. He withdrew, leaving the field to Marius, who was now temporarily in command of both his own men, that is the former survivors of Perpenna's defeat, and the present survivors of Rutilius' defeat. Perhaps because he felt that morale among his men was unsustainably low, or perhaps because he had after all not won the crushing victory attributed to him by Orosius, Marius now withdrew to Rome, taking with him for a proper funeral the dead whom he had retrieved from the battlefield.

As it turned out, in bringing back the bodies Marius did Rome a great service, for it brought the reality of war home to the people of the city. At the time however, Marius received no thanks for doing so. The sight of the fallen consul and the bodies of his officers made a demoralizing sight. 'It was a piteous spectacle, and the mourning went on for many days' says Appian. The senate decreed that thereafter, even if it was possible for the bodies of the fallen to be brought back to Rome, they should instead be interred on the battlefield. The Italians decided that this was a sensible measure and once they heard of it they passed a similar resolution. But in Rome the damage had been done – the corpses of Rutilius and his men could not be un-seen, and this was to prove of vital importance in turning the population against the war and toward the previously unpalatable measures required for peace.

Chapter 7

Surrender – an Odd Way to Win

B ecause the consul Caesar had his hands full with coping with the rebellion in the south, it was not possible for him to return to Rome to supervise the election of a replacement consul for the fallen Rutilius. Therefore it appeared that command of the northern sector would fall by default to Marius.

Then the gloomy mood in Rome induced by the display of the fallen from the battle of the Tolenus river was abruptly lightened by reports of a Roman victory. Caepio had scored a success over the Paeligni, a rebel tribe related to the Marruncini in east central Italy. All we have by way of detail is a terse observation by the epitomater of Livy[1] that 'Servius [Servilius Caepio] routed the Paeligni'. This information was enough for the senate to take sole command of the northern front away from Marius and make Caepio and Marius the co-commanders, a decision made all the easier by the fact that most senators were unhappy about giving Marius sole command because they never liked him in the first place. How Marius felt about this, history does not record. Nor did Caepio's elevation matter much in the long run, because the Italians were delighted to be opposing someone more impetuous and gullible than the cautiously suspicious Marius. They promptly set up a daring test to see just how credulous Caepio actually was. Appian takes up the story:

The opposing general, Q. Pompaedius [Silo] deserted to Caepio (though this was a pretence). As a pledge of his sincerity he brought with him his own two sons (or so he pretended. They were in fact slave babies dressed with the purple-bordered garments of free-born children.) As further confirmation of his good faith he brought masses of gold and silver (which were actually lead, plated with precious metal.)

Pompaedius pointed out that with his 'defection' his own army was currently leaderless. If Caepio made haste and followed him he could capture the entire enemy force. Completely deceived, Caepio followed to where Pompaedius said the army would be. This army was in fact hidden in ambush, and when Pompaedius ran up a hill as though to look for his men, this was the signal for them to spring from concealment. Caepio was cut to pieces, and so were most of his men.

Appian, *Civil Wars* 1.44

By default, this débâcle left Marius in sole command of the northern front against the rebellion. He had an army now composed of the remnants of Perpenna's defeated force, the remnants of Rutilius' defeated army, and the survivors of the massacre that had killed Caepio. During the weeks that followed, Marius was accused of being battle-shy even by his own exceptionally low standards. Given the tattered morale of the men he commanded, not only was it commendable of Marius to avoid putting their fragile morale to the test immediately, it was quite an achievement just to keep that army intact in the field. An incident related by Marius' biographer Plutarch probably dates to this period. It seems that Marius had managed to outmanoeuvre the enemy, but his men retreated instead of attacking. This allowed the enemy to back off undamaged from the confrontation. Marius afterwards upbraided his men with the comment 'It's hard to tell if you or the enemy are the bigger cowards. They didn't get to see your backs only because they had turned theirs to you.'[2]

When Marius was finally ready to advance, the Marsi were prepared, and had their allies the Marruncini in attendance. Shadowing the Marruncini was Sulla, who thus found himself forced to work in tandem with his old commander. Whatever their personal differences, the pair were perhaps the best generals of their day, and they proved it yet again. We do not know the details, but it appears that Marius, as was his wont, goaded the enemy into attacking him on ground that favoured the wily Roman commander. Thereafter the Italians were forced into retreat, and found Sulla waiting. The disorganized Italians were forced to change their angle of retreat into an area of vineyards surrounded by high stone walls from which it was as impossible to escape as it was to organize a defence. If the first major action at the Tolenus had been at best a draw and at worse a defeat, here the Romans avenged both this and the ambush that had killed Caepio. Some 6,000 Marsi and Marruncini were slain, along with the Marruncine general Herius Asinus. The Marsi were infuriated by the defeat, but though they raised another army, they did not yet dare put it in the field. Meanwhile the leaderless Marruncini retreated, presumably taking Sulla in pursuit, and Marius who was 65 and feeling the effects of a vigorous campaign, lapsed into inactivity. (What became of Alba Fucensis is unrecorded, but it is generally believed that the city finally surrendered around the end of the year.)

There was still plenty of life left in the war, as demonstrated by events on the southern front. Just as the stress of campaigning was taking its toll on Marius, the consul Caesar was also feeling the strain. For a while now Caesar had been forced to do his campaigning from a litter. This severely limited what he was able to do in person, and one of the things most Roman generals liked to do for themselves was to inspect the land that their armies were to cross. To make things worse for Caesar, he had lost his Numidians and their invaluable scouting skills. This made the Romans vulnerable to ambush, especially as the mountainous country of central Italy made it inevitable that an army on the march was at some point exposed to attack.

At Mons Massicus in the Volturnus valley on the road to Aesernia the predictable ambush was duly sprung. Marius Egnatius attacked from cover as the Roman army made its way through a rocky defile. Since this was not a completely unexpected development, the Roman army managed to fight its way out of the trap. The legionaries struggled towards the nearby town of Teanum, which occupied a highly defensible position. The problem was that, by definition, defensible positions are hard to approach. The only approach to Teanum lay over the pons Campanus, a narrow bridge over the river Savo, and by harrying the rearguard mercilessly, the Italians gave their Roman enemies little time to negotiate this bottleneck. The result for the Romans was a mitigated disaster. Caesar lost some 8,000 of his 30,000 infantry, but the army and its infirm commander had a safe haven to hole up in while they recovered and waited for reinforcements.

Once these reinforcements arrived, Caesar hurried to Acerrae, which was still besieged by the Italians. Caesar's earlier success in throwing back the attack on his camp had given the city time to stock up on supplies and reinforce its defences. But without help Acerrae could not hold out indefinitely, and it was a key element in the Roman defence strategy in Campania. Like the Roman army of which they had recently been a part, the Italians besieging Acerrae had made themselves a secure camp, and Caesar himself had earlier given an object lesson on the folly of assaulting one of these. The Italians had learned that lesson too, and once Caesar had established his own camp, they left it strictly alone. A sort of three-way stalemate followed. The Italians and Romans were secure in their own camps and the people of Acerrae secure behind their walls, but none of these groups had the strength to budge the other from its secure position. And so the position remained as the last days of the campaign season drew to a close, and Caesar returned to Rome to resume the struggle on the political front.

Overall, the rebels had as much reason to feel pleased with themselves as the Romans had to be worried. In the field the Italians had shown that they were more than a match for Rome's supposedly invincible armies. The Italians had made territorial gains in southern Campania while bloodying Roman noses when they attempted to poke them into Marsic territory or around Asculum. One way or another, a number of Roman and Latin settlements had fallen into Italian hands while the Italians had not lost a single settlement of any significance. Perhaps the only bad news was that Pompeius Strabo's army had broken out of confinement in Firmum on the Picentine coast, and had driven away Italian reinforcements by attacking them simultaneously in the front and rear. Now it seemed that Asculum, where the rebellion had originally broken out, was going to be the first Italian city to endure the same experience of being besieged which they had inflicted on so many of Rome's allies.

Nevertheless, Asculum was in a strong site and was well provisioned. The Italians had a number of promising sieges of their own under way that might yet add to their number of captured towns as the winter wore on, while the Romans had no gains to show for their year's campaign and a frighteningly long butcher's bill of slain citizens, including a consul, a praetor and an ex-consul. To add to Roman worries, the fact that the rebellion had grown stronger rather than being promptly quashed had been noted with interest in Etruria and Umbria. These areas had seen no fighting, but the struggle for hearts and minds was intense, and the Romans had a sinking feeling that they were losing this battle too. In the later part of the second century Roman arrogance had become a by-word in the Mediterranean basin. The Roman people expected victory as a right, and refused to abandon any struggle that did not end with the defeat or surrender of their opponents. Yet it was beginning to dawn on even the most enthusiastic of Rome's allies that this time around the Romans were in danger of losing their war. The Italians were not a barbarian people easily outmanoeuvred and out-fought by superior Roman army and logistics. Nor could the Roman army rely on the contempt the legionaries felt for 'Graeculi' (little Greeks) or decadent 'orientals'. In foreign wars this feeling, however misplaced, had translated to a real advantage of morale on the battlefield. But the legionaries knew the Samnites and Marsi from fighting alongside them, and knew there was nothing contemptible about their opponents. In terms of fighting ability the rebels actually seemed to have the edge.

This is because war was essentially one of the rebels attempting to capture or destroy the Roman colonies on their lands. Therefore the rebels were essentially operating in their home territory as they laid siege to the colonies. To lift a siege the Romans had to venture on to land the rebels knew intimately. This partly explains why the attempts to relieve besieged cities were uniformly unsuccessful, and why, with two equally matched sides the Italians had the more victories to show for the year. Through 90 BC, Rome's relative lack of success had translated into a propaganda disadvantage. It began to look as though, for all its arrogant self-confidence, Rome might after all be beaten. As that view grew in popularity among those still on the Roman side there developed a very real danger that come spring in 89 BC Umbria and parts of Etruria might abandon the Roman cause and join the rebellion. As Appian reports:

> While these events took place on the other side of Italy, the peoples of Etruria, Umbria and surrounding places heard of them and sentiment for revolt was whipped up. The senate feared they would be surrounded by war, and helpless to protect themselves.
>
> Appian, *Civil War* 1.49

It was a very real fear. If Etruria went, then Rome's already over-stretched armies would struggle to hold Campania in the south where already manpower shortages had led to ex-slaves being recruited to man the defences of Capua and the coastal cities. With Umbria too in revolt, Rome would be cut off from the reinforcements that the ever-able Quintus Sertorius was supplying from Cisalpine Gaul. Already the Gallic Saluvii on the other side of the Alps had become dangerously restive. Should the Italian tide gain momentum by the end of 89 BC 'Roman Italy' might consist of northern Picenum and Latium – and may have ceased to exist altogether by 88.

When Caesar returned to Rome from Campania to hold elections for the consuls of the following year, he found a desperately worried city. The willingness to compromise, which Livius Drusus had found so sadly lacking in 91, was suddenly there for Caesar to work with. It may have been at the point of a sword, but the Roman senate and people had indeed finally got that point. The senate's members were well informed enough to know that strategically they were in a poor position, and politically aware enough to know that Etruria was trembling on the brink. The common people might have been more reluctant to share their prized citizenship, but here Marius had done the senate an inadvertent favour. By displaying the corpses of the war dead from the battle of Tolenus in Rome, he had forced the Roman people to confront the grim reality of what their obstinacy was costing the city. There was little senatorial or popular resistance to Caesar's final act as consul, which was to pass the Lex Julia, a law that gave Roman citizenship to any Italian with the Latin Right, and made eligible for the citizenship any other Italians who were not currently killing Romans to get it. In short the Roman senate and people conceded the very point on which the rebellion was based.

This marked the turning point of the war. Up to this point Rome had been losing and was in actual danger of extinction. In effect Rome saved itself by giving what the enemy was demanding, though the Romans were not prepared to actually give the citizenship to the enemy – yet. The fact that the Lex Julia specifically excluded communities in revolt shows that the legislation was particularly aimed at keeping Etruria and Umbria on the Roman side. And this it did, though it was a close-run thing. It is clear that agitators from Asculum had been busy in their attempts to seduce both regions to the rebel cause. The Italian rebels had already prepared a flying column which would come in from the Adriatic coast to reinforce an Etrurian rebellion when it happened in spring.

On the news that Rome had offered the Etrurians citizenship this column set out in the dead of winter. Presumably the hope was that a rebel army on Etruscan soil might yet make a convincing counter-argument to the Lex Julia. After all, why accept Roman citizenship if that simply meant going down in defeat along with the rest of Rome? Fifteen thousand men set out in the column. The route over the Apennines was long and difficult even in summer. In winter the difficulty was compounded, even without the intervention of Pompeius Strabo. Strabo had been elected consul for 89 on the basis of his success at breaking out of Firmum at the end of the campaigning season of 90. Now he justified the faith the Romans had placed in him by attacking the column and killing 5,000 rebels. This attack dispersed the rebel force and around another 5,000 men died miserably in the trackless mountain wastes as they struggled to survive on windfall acorns and the gleanings remaining from autumn. The historian Orosius tells the striking story on one such detachment taking a stand on a mountain side where they died from exposure. 'Some leaned on tree stumps or rocks, others on their weapons. Their eyes were open and their teeth bared. They appeared alive and only the fact that they remained so immobile betrayed to more distant observers that they were actually dead.'[3]

So one of Rome's consuls had provided a propaganda victory to present to the Etrurians along with the citizenship. For their other consul the Romans elected Porcius Cato, a commander already on the ground in Etruria, ready with an army to provide a very practical reason why the Roman offer of citizenship should not be rejected. For Cato, news of the Lex Julia came in the nick of time, for though Cato was kept busy coping with disturbances in the region, being given the citizenship proved sufficient to keep the Etrurians from a full-scale uprising. It would also appear that the people of Umbria had been watching events in Etruria closely. Had Etruria rebelled, Umbria would probably have gone to the rebel side as well. As it was, Etruria chose to become Roman and Umbria did the same.

The Lex Julia applied specifically to communities. Each Italian city had to convene a meeting and formally pass a decree announcing that it was now Roman. This showed careful forethought. A city could not become Roman willy-nilly by default. The people had to stand up and explicitly declare themselves. And every time a city declared itself Roman, it put more pressure on neighbouring cities to do the same. In short, the Romans leveraged the desire for the citizenship in most cities against a minority of Etrurians who wanted to be shot of Rome altogether. Thus the Lex Julia had the different factions in the cities of Etruria and Umbria in competition against each other. This was 'divide and conquer' – the patented Roman technique of bringing enemy confederations to defeat. Now that the sticking point of granting citizenship had been overcome, Rome's politicians had something to do their dividing with, and they used it with enthusiasm. Two tribunes next passed an eponymous law that built on the observed effects of the Lex Julia on wavering communities. However, while the Lex Julia focused on communities, the Lex Plautia Papia was aimed at individuals. A sub-provision of the Lex Julia had already granted citizenship to any Italian from wherever so long as he was serving with distinction in Rome's armies. So now the Lex Plautia Papia took this a step further.

Any Italian, so long as he was domiciled in Italy and was on the electoral roll of an allied city – and no matter what side that city was currently on – could make a personal application to become a Roman by applying personally to the Praetor in Rome within the next sixty days. Or to put it another way, those Italians who wanted the citizenship that most of them were in rebellion to get could now obtain it by downing spears and reporting to Rome before the start of the next campaigning season. This legislation is generally seen as being aimed at community leaders and opinion-formers in the various Italian cities. However, the cynic might note that once an average peasant soldier had reported to Rome and become a Roman, he was now eligible for recruitment into a Roman legion. The Lex Plautia Papia was not just designed to split communities into Roman and rebel factions, it was also a handy recruiting tool.

As the war launched into its second campaigning season, it became clear how desperate Rome was for new recruits. Marius had failed to follow up on the success he had won in conjunction with Sulla. In part he did not trust his own men, and also his own health was suspect. Accordingly he steadfastly refused to engage the enemy, probably reasoning that an undefeated army in the field still tied up resources the Italians needed elsewhere, whereas if he gambled on a battle he might lose his demoralized men to an Italian army that would then be free to wreak havoc elsewhere.

> He never allowed the enemy to get to grips with him. He bided his time and shrugged off insults and challenges. We are told that Publius [Pompaedius] Silo, the greatest and most powerful of the enemy once challenged him 'So if you are such a great general, Marius, why not come down [from your fortifications] and fight it out?' To this Marius retorted 'Well, if you think you are any good as a general, why don't you try to make me?'
>
> Plutarch, *Life of Marius* 33

While Pompeius Strabo was able to bulk up his army from the rich recruiting grounds of Picenum, his fellow consul Cato discovered that his only recruits available to him were those who had been recalled to the standards after serving their time. These men were not particularly pleased at having to return to the army, and were truculent about doing so – even with their commanding officer.

> The men were somewhat too old to be serving in the legions, and at best Cato could exercise little authority over them. They did not obey orders readily, and were not prepared to be worked hard. When Cato dared to rebuke them for this he was practically buried under the shower of missiles they threw at him. If stones had been available, he would certainly have been killed. But the men were mustered on a soggy ploughed field, so Cato survived the clods of earth unharmed.
>
> Fragment of Cassius Dio 31.100

Having finished his stint as consul, Lucius Caesar had handed over to his successors and departed for Picenum where he served as the legate (second-in-command) to Pompeius Strabo. The situation in Picenum was very different from a few months ago when Pompeius had been holed up in Firmum. Since then a reinforcing Italian army had been beaten off, the flying column to Etruria had been destroyed and the grant of citizenship to

Roman allies and neutrals kept formerly potential allies of Asculum out of the fray. Caesar kept Asculum under siege, but the same ill-health that had dogged him through his southern campaign against the Samnites forced him to hand over command and retire to Rome.[4] The Romans later rewarded his dogged service for their cause by making him censor, the most honourable office of all the Roman magistracies.

The rebel cause in southern Picenum was led by one Vidacilius.[5] This man gathered together eight cohorts, or just under a legion's worth of recruits. With this he marched to the relief of Asculum. He sent word ahead that the people of the city should prepare for his arrival, and at a given signal they should sally out against the Romans even as he attacked them from the other side. However, even in Asculum the Roman tactic of divide and rule had its effect. There were some who hoped that by disavowing the rebel cause they might yet survive the war and become Roman citizens. Civil dissent paralysed the city, and when Vidacilius appeared outside Asculum's walls the vacillating populace did nothing. Vidacilius was by then committed to his attack, and by vigorous fighting he pushed his way through the siege lines of the surprised Romans and entered the city. He was well aware that all he had done by his attack was to add to the number of those already trapped within Asculum's walls, and was understandably peeved at the failure of the city to support what might otherwise have been a successful operation. Vidacilius proceeded to kill off those he felt responsible for the débâcle, but knew that he and the rebel cause in Asculum were now doomed. Accordingly he had a pile of his most flammable possessions stacked in one of the temples, and ordered his friends to join him in one last epic drinking bout. The last cupful of wine Vidacilius ever enjoyed was laced with a lethal dose of poison. As he felt the effects, Vidacilius ordered the pile ignited, and threw himself into it. It was a move (as one historian dryly puts it) 'widely admired but no-where imitated'.

Resistance outside Asculum was virtually extinguished by the 'ex-consul Sextus Caesar' (Appian's inability to tell his Sextus from his Lucius is a continual source of frustration, since his reference is to either the ex-consul Lucius, or the yet-to-be consul Sextus, but it is hard to tell which.) Some 20,000 Italians were in the process of shifting to new camp-grounds when whichever Caesar fell upon them, killing 8,000 and scattering the rest. A considerable quantity of weaponry was also seized, an indication that the former owners of this weaponry decided to abandon it in the course of returning to their homes and later registering as peaceable Roman citizens.[6]

Throughout the Italian peninsula the flames of rebellion were dying down. While a goodly number of die-hard rebels remained under arms, it was unclear what they were fighting for. If it was for the Roman citizenship, the best way to obtain this was to stop fighting. If it was to destroy Rome, this put the remaining rebels in direct opposition to those who had been fighting to become Roman. This left the idea that the different peoples were fighting for the independence of their tribe, yet this was somewhat nullified by the fact that the tribes had formed a confederation, and made Corfinium their capital, subsuming individual tribal identity into a larger whole in any case. So without a clear reason to keep going, a good many Italian rebels stopped fighting. It is hard to agree with the statement that they 'surrendered', since it was actually the Romans who had done so. After all, the senate had done exactly what the Italians had pressed Livius Drusus to make it do – give Roman citizenship to any Italian who asked for it. Once the senate had been forced by armed rebellion to abandon its resistance to this issue, there was effectively no *causus belli*. 'It was the one thing they all desired. .. . It made the loyal even more so, stiffened the wavering, and softened the enemy with the hope of receiving similar treatment.' remarks Appian.[7] What remained of the war in 89 BC was essentially a huge mopping-up operation.

This did not mean that the remaining rebels went quietly. One of the problems was that Roman commanders remained Roman aristocrats in a system where military glory went hand-in-hand with political success. Victory in battle earned many more votes than a quietly handled diplomatic solution, so Cato pushed on with his plans to invade Marsic territory in the spring. Had emissaries been sent instead, it is possible that the Marsi could have been taken out of the rebellion by negotiation. Such negotiations were commonplace at this point:

I was there when the consul Cn Pompeius [Strabo] met for talks with the Marsian leader P. Vettius Scato. ... After Scato had greeted Pompeius, Pompeius asked 'And how should I greet you?'

'At heart I am a friend, by necessity a foe' said Scato. The talks were calm, without fear or mistrust, and indeed with very little hatred. The [Italian] alliance did not want to rob us of our state but wanted to enter it as citizens.

Cicero, *Philippics* 12.27

But Cato had boasted how he would out-perform Marius, and was determined to match deeds with action, so he marched his army to the vicinity of Alba Fucensis. It is reasonably certain that the city had fallen by this time, so Cato was evidently setting himself up as the avenger of the city's defenders. It also gave the Marsi a reason to continue fighting, for discussions of eligibility for citizenship seem relatively arcane in comparison to the need to defend home and family from an invading army. They accordingly met Cato's army with an army of their own somewhere near the Fucine Lake, which gave Alba Fucensis its name. All we know of the action that followed was that Cato was killed in an attempt to storm the Marsic camp. That Cato was the driving force of the war in that part of Italy becomes clear in the aftermath of his death. That death was swiftly avenged in a series of sharp engagements by the legates Cinna and Metellus Pius (men of whom we will hear much more anon) but thereafter the Roman legates were happy to exchange arms for dialogue when the Marsi suggested peace talks. No doubt Metellus Pius and Cinna were well aware that the late Cato's army consisted mostly of reluctant soldiers who were less eager for glory than for the chance to return home intact, and they kept action to a minimum. Once the Romans stopped fighting there was little need for the Marsi to continue doing so, and the war in central Italy was allowed to die of benign neglect. By the end of the year the Marsi were a part of the Roman polity.

Asculum on the other hand had nailed its colours to the rebel mast, and in the city's case no negotiation was possible. Pompeius Strabo took the town, and executed all its leading citizens, presumably on the basis that Vidacilius had already done the same with any pro-Romans among them. Among those present at the taking of the city was Pompeius Strabo's son Gnaeus Pompey (later known as 'the Great') who was later prosecuted for helping himself to plunder that should have belonged to the state. Then with Asculum crushed, Pompeius Strabo used his position as consul to push through a Lex Pompeia that consolidated Rome's position among the tribes further north. Peoples such as the Veneto received the Latin Right, which meant that their leading men could shortly expect to become Roman citizens, and the remainder had the right to trade with Roman citizens under the protection of Roman law. Even the surviving rebels in southern Picenum eventually became Roman citizens. One interesting vignette resulting from this is that when Pompeius staged his triumph on 25 December 89 BC, among the prisoners displayed was a boy called Publius Venditius. Fifty-one years later Venditius was back in a triumphal parade in Rome, but this time being honoured as the only general of the Roman republic to triumph over the Parthians.

With Asculum fallen and the north now either pro-Roman or making itself actually Roman as fast as humanly possible, Strabo was able to turn his attention to the demoralized remnants of the rebellion further south. The Vestini and Marruncini 'surrendered' – that is they agreed to stop fighting in the expectation that the senate's offer of citizenship would be extended to them in due course – and the Paeligni so took exception to Scato's efforts to make them keep fighting that they arrested him. Scato would have been turned over to the Romans had his slave not slain him first.[8] As quickly as it had rebelled, south-eastern Italy returned to its Roman allegiance. Brundisium was relieved as Metellus Pius now advanced from central Italy and quickly brought Apulia under Roman control, forcing Pompaedius Silo to flee to his native Samnite people. These people would at least keep fighting, partly out of tribal loyalty to their leader and partly out of visceral anti-Roman sentiment.

By now Marius was out of the war. Either he had withdrawn under the pretext of ill-health because he felt his efforts to date had been under-appreciated, or because he was genuinely ill. It was certainly true that his recent efforts had been uninspired, and it may be that when his command lapsed at the end of 90 BC the government in Rome simply did not renew it. In any case, Marius was out of a job. In retirement he had plenty of time to watch his rival and ex-subordinate Lucius Sulla cover himself in glory. Sulla was now praetor and operating in the hills near Pompeii. When his opponent Cluentius pitched his camp almost on top of Sulla's own, an infuriated Sulla immediately launched an attack upon it. This attack possessed more impetuosity than planning, for in this case Sulla was living up to his publicly stated dictum that he did his best work on the spur of the moment.[9] He very nearly came to grief, but eventually prevailed thanks to some last-minute reinforcement by troops who returned from foraging.

When the two armies met in a more formal engagement the shakier morale of the Italian army betrayed its leader. Cluentius' army did not wait for the Romans to fall upon it, but began a spontaneous withdrawal toward the nearby city of Nola. Sulla followed up his unexpected win with great vigour and killed some 3,000 men before the rest of his enemies even reached the city walls. There, Nola's cautious commander only allowed the fleeing Italians to get in through a single gate, for the Romans were pressing so close behind that he feared that they would be able to push into the city on the heels of the men to whom he was giving shelter. An estimated 20,000 rebels were cut down while they queued for entry, among them Cluentius himself. Sulla did not settle down to besiege Nola, although he might have done so successfully as the city had not been planning on taking in such an influx of extra mouths to feed. Morale among Sulla's men was high and he wanted to keep up the momentum of success.

He turned on the Hirpini further north. There was already considerable pro-Roman sentiment in that rebel nation, as shown by the fact that one Minatius Magius had raised a legion from the Hirpini which was already serving on the Roman side. Sulla encouraged this sentiment by sparing those towns that surrendered to him. One hostile town that hoped for rebel reinforcements asked Sulla for time in which to consider surrender. Sulla was well aware of the reasons for the delay, and noted that the place had wooden walls so he ordered his men to spend that time preparing firewood. The moment the allotted time expired he had his men pile the firewood against the walls and ignite it. Bereft of its defences the town surrendered – but too late. Sulla plundered it anyway. With that example before them, the remaining towns quickly surrendered, and another rebel nation was back within Roman control.

Next on Sulla's agenda were the Samnites, and the Samnite commander Mutilus who had spent the previous year creating havoc in the towns around Pompeii and southern Campania. Mutilus was well aware that Sulla had him in his sights, and had prepared forces blocking Sulla's way. Except Sulla did not go that way. Eschewing the main roads he took his army by a circuitous route and arrived to find the enemy still awaiting his arrival from another direction. Mutilus' men quickly buckled from the surprise Roman attack and those who were not cut down on the spot fled in disorder. Mutilus himself was wounded, but was able to withdrew with a few followers to Aesernia. This town was well able to withstand siege, as testified by its long resistance before the Italians had captured it. Now Mutilus intended to use the town's secure defences for his own benefit. In fact Aesernia now became the *de facto* Italian base in the region, for once again Sulla declined to get bogged down in a siege and moved against Bovianum, which had been the previous Italian headquarters. Again, there was no siege. Sulla knew that he had already broken Mutilus' army and that the city had to be poorly garrisoned. He ordered his men to take whichever of the city's strong-points seemed weakest, and then used the capture of that strong-point as a springboard to take the rest of the city in a ferocious three-hour assault.

The Samnites were feeling the pressure elsewhere as well. One of Sulla's fellow praetors, Cosconius, advanced as far south as Cannae (once the site of Rome's devastating defeat at the hands of Hannibal). Here his attempt at taking the town of Canusium was prevented by Samnite relief forces who handed Cosconius a bruising defeat. The two sides ended up on opposite sides of a river, and the Samnite leader chivalrously proposed to withdraw so that the Romans could fight on his side, or alternatively that the Romans withdraw so that the Samnites could fight on the other side. Cosconius agreed to the latter proposal, but faked his withdrawal. His men caught the Samnite army in mid-crossing and wiped out 15,000 of them. Cosconius left Canusium and the remnants of the Samnite army for later and resumed his southward drive. This allowed Metellus Pius to recapture Rome's one and only rebel colony, Venusia, along with 3,000 prisoners. Meanwhile, the death in action of Marius Egnatius removed the man described by Livy as 'the most noble leader' from the rebel side.

Even worse news awaited the Samnites. With an army partly raised from freed slaves Pompaedius Silo had re-taken Bovianum from Sulla, but this was his last success. In a spirited attempt to eject Metellus from Apulia, Pompaedius Silo not only failed, but died in the attempt. So of the Italian leaders Cluentius was now wounded, Mutilus was penned up in Aesernia, Scato and Egnatius were dead and Pompaedius Silo, the 'heart and soul' of the rebellion, had just died also. It was little consolation to the rebel cause that the Romans had also lost more of their own leaders. The legate Gabinius died attempting to re-take Grumentum (which had fallen to the rebels in the previous year), and Titus Didius fell in battle shortly after he had brought Herculaneum back under Roman authority by a violent assault. Presumably Pompeii surrendered at around this time, for now only Nola and Aesernia remained in rebel hands in the south-west. The last fires of the rebellion were flickering out.

Chapter 8

Sulla's March on Rome –
this Changes Everything

With the Samnites still holding out in the field, it would be wrong to say that the Italian war was over, but the Romans could at least now feel that they had a grip on things. This was just as well, for there were other urgent matters demanding their attention, both at home and abroad. At home the Italians had discovered that the senate had partly cheated on their grant of citizenship, and from this discovery a political crisis blew up that required further hasty concessions. But the greater menace lay abroad.

Mithridates VI of Pontus had been contemplating Rome's problems in Italy with considerable interest. It was evident that with Italians and Romans locked in a life-or-death struggle there would be few legions available to fight in Asia Minor. This was just as well for the Pontic king, because Mithridates had been particularly provocative in the years leading up to 90 BC. Mithridates was eager to gain suzerainty over two neighbouring kingdoms; Cappadocia and Bithynia. In the past he had tried installing puppet rulers in Cappadocia (including his sister and young son) and had even resorted to direct invasion when less subtle forms of coercion failed. Every time he took control of the neighbouring kingdom, emissaries from Rome had arrived and told him to back off and leave Cappadocia alone. In one of these diplomatic incidents, forces sponsored by Mithridates had clashed with the governor of Cilicia, who at that time was Cornelius Sulla. Eventually Mithridates had tired of competing with Nicomedes of Bithynia for control of Cappadocia. He arranged for a palace coup to drive Nicomedes from his throne and installed a puppet king in his rival's place. He then had his son-in-law, the equally ambitious Tigranes the Great of Armenia, invade Cappadocia. Thereafter Mithridates installed another client king in

Cappadocia, and with both Cappadocia and Bithynia under his thumb, he settled back to await the inevitable Roman delegation.

Perhaps Mithridates felt that with their local difficulties in Italy, the Romans would be somewhat more conciliatory this time around. If so, he had forgotten the advice given to him by Marius (who had visited the region in the previous decade) that he should either be stronger than Rome, or do what he was told without complaint.[1] The Romans were as uncompromising as ever. Mithridates was bluntly told to put back the deposed kings of Cappadocia and Bithynia and to leave these two kingdoms alone in future.

The Romans delegation was led by one Manlius Aquillius, the former Roman consul of 101 BC. Manlius Aquillius was a Roman of the old school. That is to say he was corrupt, greedy (he had already been prosecuted for maladministration in Sicily) and incompetent. The Roman firmness that so nonplussed Mithridates was deliberately provocative, because Aquillius wanted a war. The Roman emissary knew that Pontus was an enormously rich kingdom, not least because his father had been governor of the former kingdom of Pergamon (now the Roman province of Asia), where he had become rich through the ruinously high taxes he had unjustly imposed on its peoples. The son felt that Mithridates was a paper tiger whose vaunted armies would quickly collapse under the assault of Roman troops from the province of Asia and the armies of Rome's Anatolian allies. So, with hopes of a short and profitable war before him, it was highly frustrating for Aquillius when Mithridates decided to back down while he investigated what lay behind this confident Roman approach. Both puppet rulers were displaced and the rightful kings restored to their thrones, so Aquillius was left with no pretext for war.

However, Aquillius was not going to allow his chance for wealth to slip away so easily. He intimated to Nicomedes of Bithynia that the price for his restoration to power was that he should invade Pontus. With deep reluctance, the Bithynian king did so, thus provoking a war against Pontus in which Rome, as a Bithynian ally, could legitimately participate. It should have come as a warning to the Romans when the Bithynian invasion was crushed, not by the main Pontic army but by a strong reconnaissance in force led by an opportunist Pontic commander. There proved to be nothing paper about the Pontic tiger. The army had been hardened by fighting Mithridates' wars of conquest in the kingdoms to the north of the Black Sea, and their king was intelligent, ruthless and well-prepared. The planned Roman invasion crumpled under the Pontic onslaught, and as Mithridates counter-attacked, Aquillius had to flee for his life through a countryside that jubilantly threw off Roman rule. But the Roman did get his gold in the end. Captured by local people and handed over to Mithridates, Aquillius died from gold melted to liquidity which was poured down his throat as a symbol of his greed.

It was a horrible way to die, yet one might forgive contemporary Romans for feeling that Aquillius deserved it. For personal gain he had precipitated a war that Rome had neither the men nor the resources to fight. Preoccupied by the war in Italy, the senate could do nothing as Rome was driven from Asia Minor. Then, as Mithridates followed up his conquests, Rome was forced out from much of Greece as well – and worse was to come. Even as the Romans began to get the upper hand in the Italian war, Mithridates hit upon a way of ensuring that none of the cities in his new empire would defect back to the Roman side. He arranged that every Latin in his domains, be that person Italian or Roman, was to be executed on one single day. It says something of how heartily the Romans were hated in the region that no one received the slightest warning until the massacre began, and when it did begin the killing was done with bloodthirsty enthusiasm. Between 80,000 and 150,000[2] 'Romans and Italians were killed, with their wives and children and their freedmen of Italian birth, and their bodies thrown out unburied and their goods shared.' Appian remarks 'It was very clear that these atrocities were committed every bit as much out of hatred for the Romans as from fear of Mithridates.'[3]

From the Roman perspective, if there was one redeeming feature from this entire story of greed, defeat and massacre it was that Romans and Italians had suffered equally at the hands of a common enemy. At one point, when Mithridates had first gone to war with the Romans, the Italians had considered asking Mithridates to invade Italy on their behalf.[4] Now grieving families up and down the peninsula looked to avenge loved ones who had died in the east, and they were prepared to work with Rome to do so. Yet even as shared grief and anger drove Romans and Italians together, political chicanery by the senate was pulling them apart.

In Rome, the main legislative assembly was not the senate. In fact despite its immense (though recently diminished) authority, the senate was technically only an advisory body to the Roman people. Laws were actually passed by several different assemblies of the Roman people, but most legislation went through the *concilium plebis*, and the *comitia tributa*. The '*tributa*' refers to 'tribes', although these tribes were not family-linked bands in the usual anthropological sense, but rather hereditary voting constituencies into which all new Romans were enrolled.

Over the centuries the Roman aristocracy had managed to gain control of voting in the 'tribal' assemblies. This had been done partly through patronage, which worked for both the aristocrat and his many clients among the common people. (Clients voted for laws favouring their patron because the more power a patron had, the more he could help his clients.) More blatant control was exerted through bribery, and when all else failed, through outright intimidation. One of the reasons why Marius was so unpopular with the senate was that his legislation had made it harder for the aristocracy to bully people into voting the way they 'should'. Nevertheless, through bribery of the people *en masse* and selective intimidation to keep certain groups from voting at all, the senate generally had a grip on the legislative process. That grip had slipped on occasion in previous decades when the general populace had been simply too furious with the senate to be told what to do, but despite this neither senate nor the people of Rome were enthusiastic about admitting a mass of new voters. These would be out of the control of the senate and also unlikely to vote for laws favouring those citizens living in Rome.

So as Italians gained the citizenship, new voting tribes were created for them. This had in fact been the Roman practice until 241 BC, and we can suppose the new tribes were added two at a time to keep the number uneven. (This was to prevent deadlock if the number of tribes voting for a bill exactly balanced the number voting against.) However, the new tribes would vote after the current tribes, and as with the *comitia centuriata* (which elected top Roman magistrates) once a vote had been reached by a majority, the voting was stopped. Since Rome had already thirty-five tribes, and a maximum of ten new tribes was contemplated, it was unlikely that the newcomers would have a say other than a casting vote in close decisions. Any legislation favouring the older Roman citizens would be passed as a done deal without the new citizens getting the chance to so much as vote on it.

That at least seems to have been the intention. As is often the case, our two main sources, Appian and Velleius Paterculus, are at variance here, with Appian claiming the citizens were put into ten new tribes and Velleius stating that the thousands of new citizens were jammed into just eight of the existing tribes. We even get a fragmentary contribution from Sisenna, the only historian who was actually around at the time and who is therefore the only historian who definitively knew what he was talking about. Sisenna refers to two new tribes, so it is possible that what actually happened is that the new citizens were put into eight of the old tribes of Velleius and the overflow into two new ones as per Sisenna, thus making the ten tribes that Appian believes were created. In either case we get the new citizens in ten tribes (at most) and if those tribes voted last, the existing arrangement between Roman aristocrats and voters would remain unchanged with the Italians effectively disenfranchised from legislation.

The hope must have been that the Italians would be content with having a vote in the *comitia centuriata* and with the protection of Roman law. After all, the *comitia centuriata* decided major issues such as the election of the next year's consuls and whether or not Rome should go to war, and Roman law protected a citizen anywhere in the empire. So perhaps the *novi cives* would accept a very limited say in legislation? However, after over a decade spent struggling for their rights the *novi cives* were not naïve. They knew the political process almost as well as the average Roman voter, and knew that without a say in legislation they could be slowly marginalized once again by selective legislation. For example, the question of who served on juries had recently been resolved by a law that allowed each tribe to vote for a number of jurors, whether these were commoners, equites or senators. Future legislation might 'fine-tune' the tribes that could so vote and exclude the new citizens from these juries, which would deny the Italians the very protection of the courts that they had fought so hard to gain. So the Italians were having none of it. They demanded to be registered in the existing tribes,[5] and once it was clear that the Italians would vote in electoral assemblies for whomever backed them up on this, a flock of opportunist Roman politicians hastened to announce their support for the measure.

Once the dust had settled, it is clear from the results that the senate managed to effect a compromise. The four 'urban' tribes that mostly held people who actually resided in Rome had no new citizens added to their number. Those peoples who had not rebelled were spread more or less evenly among the other tribes, which prevented them from uniting to act as a single group on any issues. However, as rebel peoples were absorbed they were each lumped into a single tribe. Though each tribe might be recalcitrant on a given issue, since there were only eight major rebel groups even if the rebels voted as a bloc, and even if they attained a majority in their own tribe, they were still too few to prevail against the rest of Italy. In fact it might be those 'eight tribes' that the slightly confused Velleius Paterculus was actually talking about.[6]

The foreign war with Mithridates and the legislative arrangements with the new citizens – the two issues seemed at first unrelated. However, as events unfolded in 88 BC they were to combine in a disastrous conjunction that made the entire Italian war merely the first part of a continuing cataclysm. The Roman aristocracy had lost many of their number in battle, including serving and former consuls. As the war slowly ran down, the survivors might have felt relief that the storm had finally passed. In fact the worst was yet to come.

Romans, both old and newly created, had three major issues to deal with in the year 88 BC. Issue one we have partly discussed, as that was the question of smoothly absorbing a huge mass of extra citizens into the Roman legislative and constitutional framework. Issue two was that of sorting out the mess from the war. An estimated 300,000 Romans and Italians had perished in the fighting, and with those on both sides in the process of becoming the same nation, there were questions of land ownership, inheritance and treaty rights to laboriously sort through and decide. Not to mention that some bits of Italy, especially the Samnites, had given up on Roman citizenship and doggedly continued to fight for independence. For this reason Sulla, one of the consuls-elect for 88 BC, aimed to leave Rome soon after the elections to continue with the immediate business on hand which was the siege to re-take Nola in Campania. Issue three was the matter of Mithridates. Thanks to him, Greece and Asia Minor were now enemy territory. It is also probable that Macedonia was lost, or at best the Roman grip had been severely weakened. These losses constituted a goodly chunk of Rome's once-growing empire, and the Romans wanted them back, not least because there was no reason to believe that the expansionist and predatory Mithridates would rest content with what he had got. So while Sulla was mopping up in Campania, the senate would busy itself with the levy for what was intended to be the main event of the year – the reconquest of the east.

At this point the Roman people were introduced to a somewhat bizarre sight. The elderly and corpulent Marius had left his luxurious home in Baiae near Misenum and now exercised daily with the young men on the Campus Martius, ignoring those who kindly advised him that he would be better off in the public baths nursing his rheumatism. Rome's old war-horse was burnishing his image with the public to put himself in the running for one last campaign. He wanted to lead the war against Mithridates. This was allegedly so that he could instruct his son in warfare; a reason that his biographer Plutarch frankly dismisses as 'silly'. The real reason was, 'He didn't understand the limits of good fortune, and was not content to enjoy what he had and to be admired for what he had done.'[7] Apart from the fact that Marius was around seventy years old and his record in the recent war was mediocre, there was one over-riding difficulty about his leading the army to war in Asia – the senate had already awarded that command to Sulla. That his rival had been given this opportunity was undoubtedly one of the reasons why Marius wanted it. He could get it too, because he had found a politician who wanted something from him in return.

P. Sulpicius Rufus was an aristocratic tribune of the plebs, and a former friend of Livius Drusus. He had started the year with a relatively unassuming legislative programme, unassuming that is, apart from one major and controversial proposal. Sulpicius wanted all new citizens to be redistributed evenly across the thirty-five tribes of Rome, and furthermore that all manumitted slaves should be enrolled on the same basis. This proposal was certainly in the spirit of Livius Drusus, and it would iron out the inequalities of the current arrangement and so was worth doing for its own sake. However, cynics also noted that this would also give Sulpicius the support of the grateful Italians and freedmen for the rest of his political career. Naturally enough the senate was appalled, as were the voters in the 'urban tribes', which were not scheduled to be diluted by new voters. Therefore

Sulpicius faced very considerable opposition to his bill. So he asked for and got the endorsement of Marius. Marius was still immensely popular with Roman voters. They remembered how as tribune he had passed laws that made voting freer, and how as consul he had defeated Jugurtha and fended off the Cimbric menace. The newly enfranchised Italians also saw Marius as sympathetic to their cause. With Marius campaigning at Sulpicius' side, there was a good chance of Sulpicius' legislation becoming law. The *quid pro quo* for Marius was another law that was to be passed immediately afterwards. This law would strip Sulla of his Asian command and transfer it to Marius.

Not unnaturally, Sulla and his allies threw themselves into the task of preventing either law from coming into force. Sulpicius was a tribune, but Sulla was a consul who had most of the senate behind him. The result was deadlock. Sulpicius might have had the votes, but before voting could take place the senate decreed an *iustitium* – an indefinite suspension of public business. It remains controversial to this day whether the senate had the right to over-rule the programme of a tribune in this way. But as Plutarch remarks 'Sulpicius was not a man of hesitation' and he was not prepared to wait for the constitutional process to resolve the issue. The tribune habitually surrounded himself with a gang of bravos whom he called his 'anti-senate' and for this occasion he also raised a militia of some 3,000 armed followers. With these he set about overturning the *iustitium* by force. Depending on one's point of view this was either a robust response to an illegal decree by the senate or it was an act of armed sedition. In either case, Sulpicius had dramatically raised the stakes and thereafter matters quickly got out of hand.

The consuls were addressing the people in the forum when Sulpicius and his men arrived and a full-scale riot quickly developed, with the senate's supporters swiftly overwhelmed by the better-prepared followers of Sulpicius. Pompeius Rufus, Sulla's co-consul, barely escaped with his life. His son (who was also Sulla's son-in-law) was not so lucky; he was butchered by the mob. Sulla himself got away by doing the unexpected. He ducked into the house of Marius, something which he explained away later – with some discomfort – by claiming he had gone to consult with his rival on the disastrous civic situation. Negotiations followed that led to Sulla going to the forum and enduring the humiliation of publicly rescinding the suspension of public business. With Sulpicius now the master of Rome, both his laws were briskly voted through. Marius had his army, and Sulla took himself back to the siege of Nola, which was now his only remaining military business of the year.

What happened next, as Plutarch perceptively remarks 'brought to a head the secret disease from which the state had long been suffering'. In essence, the problem was that the ancient constitution of Rome no longer reflected the current circumstances. In the past the Roman voter and the Roman soldier had been essentially the same person. If the Roman assemblies had voted for the commander of an army, the voters in that assembly were the same men who would later serve in that army under that commander. This was no longer the case. Anyone wanting to vote had to do so in Rome, in person. It was one thing if a citizen felt strongly enough about an issue that he had to travel to Rome to make his voice heard, but it was completely another issue if a citizen could not travel to Rome and vote there because he was already serving his country elsewhere as a soldier.

It was always galling for the army to find that it had voted an incompetent to command it, but at least the voters in the army had done that to themselves. Now the Romans in the army found that people in Rome (who did not have to do the fighting) had voted them a general whom they did not want and had thrown out the general that they did. A gap had opened between the Roman voter and the Roman soldier, effectively disenfranchising the latter. This 'secret disease' had been made all the more virulent by the recent war, as the legions now contained soldiers who had never even voted (because the censors had not yet got around to putting them on the voter's roll). The soldiers gathered for the Asian campaign expressed their opinion of the Roman voters and of Sulpicius' legislation by lynching the officers sent by Marius to take over. With that mutiny it became clear that Marius did not have his army after all. But Sulla had one, and he was bringing it to Rome.

Sulla had been publicly humiliated, and he was not the forgiving kind. He had been born of a noble yet impoverished family and unlike many of his contemporaries had reached his current position through a combination of luck, hard work and ability – ironically, characteristics that he shared with Marius. Because Marius had been forced to fight so hard for what he had achieved he was constitutionally unable to rest on his laurels. If that meant Sulla had to lose out, then, given Marius' jealous disposition, that was something of a bonus. However, Sulla had fought just as hard to get to where he was, and he was not going to let Marius take it all away – and the fact that Marius had made a promising start at doing so made him all the more grimly furious. Sulla's argument to the army appealed to a mixture of patriotism and greed. Asia was immensely rich, and plundering its cities was practically a duty after the peoples of those cities had massacred Romans and Italians by the tens of thousands.

Yet if Marius took control of the campaign, he would go with his own officers, and any Sullan loyalists would be shouldered aside and like their erstwhile commander, left at the siege of Nola. And there was Rome itself, currently run by a demagogic tribune who used the mob to over-rule the senate and was prepared to kill anyone – including a consul's son – who stood in his way. Again, it was the duty of the army as soldiers and good citizens to proceed to Rome and put matters right. It is improbable that either Sulla or his men saw what they were doing as a power-grab or a coup. If anything, they felt that the coup had been already accomplished. Sulpicius had taken control of the city by violence and the army was needed to restore legitimate government.

Yet this was no longer true. The senate had indeed been subject to the dictates of Marius and Sulpicius, but on the news that Sulla was marching on the city with six legions, senate and people came together in the face of the impending threat. Even all of Sulla's own officers apart from one quaestor were so horrified by Sulla's intentions that they left the army and fled to Rome. There, the senate sent two praetors to inform Sulla that his march on Rome was forbidden. By an effort Sulla prevented his over-enthusiastic army from lynching the praetors, but their fasces, the symbols of their authority, were broken and the praetors' senatorial togas were stripped from them. If ever Romans needed a graphic image of the way things would be from now onwards, this was it. The army had indeed broken the power of the senate and stripped it of its authority, and the coming decades would prove this again and again.

When Sulla and his army arrived outside Rome, it was clear he was not bluffing. A further delegation came from the senate and Sulpicius bearing notice of surrender. The senate had voted that Sulla would have 'all his rights' – a phrase presumably including Sulla's restoration to the command of the war against Mithridates. But Sulla did not just want his rights, he wanted revenge. Furthermore he suspected that the capitulation was a ruse to gain time in which the city might be further fortified against an assault. Accordingly Sulla pretended to accept the senate's capitulation while he sent a speedy advance party to capture the gates and the walls near the Esquiline hill. The people of the Esquiline fought back, but roof-tiles and brickbats were little use against determined veteran soldiers – especially after Sulla threatened to burn down the houses beneath the tile-throwers.

To get his way against the senate Sulpicius had raised the stakes by bringing in the mob. Sulla had not backed down but raised the stakes again by bringing in the army. Now Sulpicius and Marius tried to raise the stakes again by promising freedom to any slaves who joined the impromptu army they were trying to raise to defend the city. This was a mistake. Firstly because even if every slave in the city heeded the call for freedom (and the vast majority sensibly did not), it is unlikely that they could have prevailed against veteran legionaries, so Sulla's grip on the city would have remained firm, even if more bloodstained. But more importantly, attempting to raise a slave rebellion was a capital crime. Marius and Sulpicius would already have to face charges of overthrowing the authority of the consuls by violence and of collusion in the murder of the consul's son. To this was now added the offence of outright sedition because (according to Appian at least), Marius and Sulpicius had led whatever troops they could muster into combat against Sulla's men 'not in factional mob fighting, but with regular troops under military standards ordered by trumpet call'.[8]

Mob violence, lynching, armed rebellion and attempting to raise a slave rebellion: these were the charges that Sulla invited the senate to consider against Marius, Sulpicius and their followers. There was also the fact that the perpetrators had chosen not to face the victor's justice – they had fled rather than argue their case. Sulla was completely in control, as proven by his summary treatment of those enterprising soldiers who tried a bit of freelance looting and pillaging. Like the rest of Rome, the senate was completely cowed, and passed a decree declaring Marius, Sulpicius and Marius' son to be enemies of the state. Sulpicius was quickly disposed of – he was found hiding in a villa after one of his own slaves betrayed him to the informers who were already on his track. Typically, Sulla rewarded the slave as promised, then had him killed for the betrayal of his master's trust. Marius was harder to track down. Rome's six-time consul remained a popular hero to many. Few had yet realized exactly how vindictive Sulla could be, so they were prepared to give the fleeing ex-consul food and shelter. In Rome Sulpicius' legislation was decreed as invalid, having been passed *per vim* – that is, through violence. Sulla had a keen sense of irony and was no doubt aware of it in the fact that he had applied no little violence of his own in getting his opponent's laws disqualified.

At this point Sulla had few friends outside his army; a fact that he blithely pretended to ignore. As was his duty as consul, Sulla held the elections for his successor. He pretended to be pleased that his own candidates were rejected out of hand by an electorate that was at pains to vote for those candidates most calculated to annoy him. This, Sulla accurately pointed out, showed democracy in action. He was, however, able to secure the election of one Octavius as consul. Octavius was a steady character and a solid supporter of Sulla, and therefore a vital counter-balance to the other man elected as consul, Lucius Cinna, a firebrand who was violently opposed to everything Sulla was and had done. Having made the two new consuls swear to keep the peace, Sulla took himself and his army off to Greece. As far as he was concerned going to campaign against Mithridates was the whole point of the exercise, yet he can hardly have been unaware of the far-reaching significance of his actions.

Basically, Rome had been conquered. True, it had been conquered by a duly elected consul with a properly levied army, but that was hardly the point. While Sulla had both reason and excuse, what he had done could be done again with less reason and no excuse, provided that the soldiers felt strongly enough about it. That army was no longer a corps of soldiers born and raised on the seven hills of Rome. Now, a legionary might as easily come from Milan, or from Brundisium half a thousand miles away, or from anywhere in between. For these soldiers the right to a vote in Rome was meaningless. Yet – as the contretemps over the command of the Mithridatic war had proven – the decisions of the Roman electorate could have a very marked effect on every soldier's life. Now that the Roman electorate was no longer representative of the Roman army, what Sulla's coup had done (and despite everything, it was indeed a coup) was to assert the army's primacy over the Roman voter in decision making. Once this primacy had been asserted, there was no going back, and to a very real extent, the Roman Republic after 88 BC was a sham. In reality, Rome was a military dictatorship that had just not realized it yet.

Just to prove that Sulla was a symptom rather than a cause of the problem, once he was out of the way and campaigning against Mithridates in Greece, Roman democracy did not settle down, but instead went to hell in a handcart. Cinna had sworn to keep the peace and to recognize the settlement that Sulla had imposed on Rome. Yet barely had Sulla left the premises than Cinna broke his promise and began to undo Sulla's work. The firebrand consul announced that he intended to revive all the legislation of Sulpicius that Sulla had overturned, and hinted at plans to prosecute Sulla for his actions. Naturally enough, this was opposed by Octavius and the conservative element among both the senate and voters in Rome. When the matter came to the vote, a tribunican veto was interposed. Now so far, the situation was working as the Roman constitution was supposed to. That is, the consuls were deadlocked with opposing programs and a tribune had prevented the matter from going any further. This is why all Roman magistracies were collegial. If those in office could not work together, then the system was devised so that they should not work at all. However, Cinna was not prepared to leave matters at that. He tried, as had Sulpicius before him, to use the mob to push through his legislation. However, this time the conservatives were prepared, and Cinna's faction lost the ensuing riot. Then like Marius before him, Cinna called for a slave rebellion – and when that failed, he fled the city.

Like a true traditionalist, Octavian now used constitutional forms. He proposed decrees in the senate that declared Cinna a public enemy and a replacement consul was chosen. For Octavius the crisis was now over. Cinna had a better grasp of the new reality, and once expelled from Rome, he started to look for an army. Already a corps of anti-Sullan dissidents was beginning to form around him. One member was Sertorius, the man who had done so well in feeding a steady supply of Gallic recruits to Rome's armies during the recent war. Another was Marius Gratidianus, a nephew of the exiled Marius. These men arrived at the camp of the commander of the Roman army in Campania, and through rousing speeches to the men, basically hijacked the commander's army from under him.

Marius had escaped to Africa. There had been a close shave at Minturnae, where Marius had been captured, but no one was prepared to kill Rome's former hero. Not sure what else to do with him, the Minturnians put Marius on a ship and (after another near-death experience in Sicily), Marius had ended up skulking near Carthage when news reached him of developments in Italy. When he heard that Cinna had found an army and was marching on Rome, Marius hastened to join in. It is questionable to what extent he was still sane. Certainly his close encounters with death while on the run had affected him deeply, and Marius had spent much of his time in exile brooding on real and imagined wrongs. On his arrival in Italy he raised recruits by offering freedom to slaves and by professing devotion to the legislative program of Sulpicius, but he was really fixated on revenge – the bloodier the better. Cinna professed to be delighted at having a person so venerated join his side, but Sertorius and others had their reservations even before Marius captured Ostia – a sensible measure that cut off Rome's food supply – and then pillaged the place and killed most of the inhabitants, apparently because he could. For the first time, a Roman town was treated by a Roman general as if it were enemy territory.

The battle lines were taking shape. Belatedly, Octavius had realized that the matter would be settled with force rather than senatorial decrees, and had found an unlikely ally in Pompeius Strabo, the general who had defended Picenum for Rome in the civil war. Like Sulla, Pompeius Strabo had an army that was loyal to himself rather than to Rome, and this army too had proven its contempt for the central authority by lynching the man sent to relieve Pompeius Strabo of his command. This lynching was now politely ignored by Octavius who was desperate for manpower. Even with the fill-up provided by Pompeius Strabo's army Octavius still needed more men. Consequently he had the senate pass a decree enfranchising any of those Italians who were still fighting against Rome on the sole condition that those men now fought on the conservative side instead. Since the franchise had previously been given only to those not actually in arms against the Romans, this decree was welcomed by a number of rebel Italians who realized that their war was now a lost cause. This number did not include the Samnites, who ambushed and savaged a large group of defectors from their cause. Metellus Pius, the son of Metellus Numidicus (p.31), brought the rest to

Rome, but their number was more than balanced by the Samnites who went over to the Cinnan side. Thus the embers of the Italian war came to life again and merged with the new conflagration.

Rome was besieged, but capably defended by Octavius and Pompeius Strabo. We know few details of the actual siege, but it is clear the defenders of the city were greatly outnumbered. Then Pompeius Strabo died at the crucial moment; probably of illness, though Appian says he was struck by lightning.[9] His death left the defenders with a major problem because Pompeius' men despised Octavius and refused to serve under him. The only other credible general, Metellus Pius, punctiliously refused to replace the consul in command. Wholesale desertions to the Cinnans quickly resolved the impasse, for Octavius quickly ran out of an army with which to defend the city. He was forced into unconditional surrender. For the second time in two years, Rome had fallen to a Roman army. Yet the two conquests were not the same. Sulla maintained to the end that he was a consul restoring order in the city after an outbreak of mob rule. Whatever his inclinations, apart from punishing those he considered guilty of inciting that mob rule, he had refrained from vengeance. Vengeance, on the other hand was what Marius was all about. Guilt or innocence had little to do with it. His intention was not to restore order, but to make sure that those whom he considered as having betrayed him now paid for it with their lives.

Octavius was lynched in front of the senate house before Marius had even entered Rome. The consul had refused to abandon the city, and stayed at his post until he was killed. His head was cut off and displayed on a spear at the nearby rostra – the start of a grim tradition that was often to be emulated in the dying republic. Marius was not yet present for the occasion because he pretended that as an exile he had no right to enter Rome before the people voted for his recall. A frightened populace immediately assembled and began voting, but by then Marius had grown impatient with the charade and entered anyway, accompanied by a bodyguard of freed slaves, which he called 'the Bardyaei'.

These thugs needed only the word of command before they summarily slew Roman citizens. In fact sometimes it took a mere nod. Finally Ancharius, a man of senatorial and praetorian rank, met Marius. When his salutation received no reply, this was considered enough of a signal for the man to be cut down right there in the street. As a result, even friends of Marius were filled with fear and horror when they came to greet him. As the killing went on, Cinna lost his appetite for the slaughter, but the thirst of Marius for blood would not be sated. Day after day his anger increased and he killed anyone whom he had ever suspected of anything.

Plutarch, Life of Marius 44

Among the casualties was Lutatius Catulus, the man who some fifteen years before had the impertinence to defeat the Cimbri in a battle in which Marius had played the lesser part. Now Catulus paid for taking a share of the glory, despite pleas even from Marian supporters that an ex-consul who had shared a triumph with Marius deserved well of the state. All Marius would stubbornly reply was 'He must die'; and so Catulus did.[10] There were other casualties among those senators who did not wisely make an early escape. Metellus Pius was among the latter, and also Licinius Crassus (the man who was later to be a triumvir along with Julius Caesar and Pompey). Others were saved by friends or even slaves, such as an aristocrat called Cornutus, whose servants dressed a suitable corpse (there were plenty to choose from) as their master and burned it. Sulla's wife and family escaped, though not without risk. However, one redeeming feature of the late Republic is that for all the mayhem unleashed on their menfolk, the women were considered as outside the political struggle and we do not hear of any losing their lives. However, Sulla's property was declared forfeit and the vindictive Marius had his house razed to the ground even as he continued to hunt down and kill anyone suspected of being Sulla's friend.

While Marius was decorating the rostra with the heads of slain aristocrats, his Bardyaei were losing his faction support among the common people. 'They slaughtered fathers in their own homes, and violated the wives and children in an unchecked rampage of rape and murder' reports Plutarch.[11] Fortunately, given their conduct, the Bardyaei had to all sleep in one place for mutual protection, since the outraged Romans would have torn to pieces any member of the group they caught alone. This made it easy for Cinna and Sertorius to have armed men surround the open ground where the Bardyaei were encamped. After a sustained shower of javelins had rained down on the sleeping men, Rome had one less problem to worry about.

Nor was Marius to long outlive his Bardyaei. At the start of the new year, he became consul for a record-breaking seventh time, an event celebrated by another supposed enemy of Marius being thrown to his death from the Tarpean rock on the Capitoline hill. Worn out by the exertions and stress of the previous year, Marius died within the first month of his latest consulship. He had managed to demonstrate the point that he had indeed been totally unfit for the command of the Mithridatic War which had sparked off this latest crisis, but by then few of Sulla's supporters were alive in Rome to tell Cinna 'I told you so'. Exactly how many perished in this bout of blood-letting is unknown, for the historians of the time are more concerned with rhetorical expressions of outrage than with supplying an exact body-count. It is, however, very clear that the occupation of the city by the army of Marius and Cinna was an altogether grimmer business than the occupation by Sulla had been. Within months Rome had gone from a city ruled by law and constitution to a city under mob rule, followed by army occupation under Sulla, followed by siege and conquest by Marius and Cinna and a subsequent reign of terror. Not just the people of the city, but Romans across the empire must have asked themselves how this could have come about.

One reason was that all concerned were Romans, and the Romans of the republic were very bad at compromise. The response of a Roman to a setback was to raise the stakes and try again, and to keep escalating the situation until his opponent backed down. This worked well enough with more reasonable peoples in Greece and even the rest of Italy, but when Roman confronted Roman matters could get very quickly out of hand. The senate had refused to negotiate with the Gracchus brothers, even though doing so would have defused the coming crisis a generation before it broke. The senate had also refused to contemplate the legislative program of Livius Drusus in 91 BC, even though this represented the last chance to avert war and the loss of hundreds of thousands of lives. Only when the alternative was extinction did the senate and people of Rome finally back down, but by then the political process had been contaminated and coarsened by violence, and men accustomed to warfare were less patient with the inevitable setbacks, compromises and back-room deals that are an unavoidable part of peacetime politics. When Sulpicius, Sulla and Cinna were thwarted, they instinctively resorted to the violence that had been their stock-in-trade since the outbreak of the Italian war.

Yet now with the death of Marius, peace of a sort broke out. Or at least what Cicero refers to as the *triennium sine armis* or 'three years without warfare' – a rare event in a bloody decade. Warfare there was, of course. But it happened overseas in Greece where, despite being declared a public enemy and stripped of his command and funding for his army, Sulla continued to successfully prosecute the war against Mithridates. There was not a lot that the government in Rome could do about this, because Sulla's army could handily support itself on the land, and Sulla kept the men paid by taking the sacred treasures of Delphi into 'safe-keeping'. The senate could and did send out an army of its own to campaign in the east, but in a sad reflection of the times, its commander was killed by an ambitious subordinate called Fimbria. Rome now had two armies in the east, each of dubious loyalty, but at least committed to fighting Mithridates. At home in Italy, peace of a sort prevailed. Overall, by the standards of recent years, this was definitely progress.

Chapter 9

Sulla's Return – Fighting for Rome

While Sulla was away campaigning against Mithridates an uneasy calm prevailed. With the fortuitous death of Marius a semblance of normal government returned to Rome. Cinna pushed through a badly needed debt relief programme which, not incidentally, further secured for himself the loyalty of the common people. He also took sensible steps to deal with a currency crisis caused by Livius Drusus' debasement of the coinage and the financial ravages of the Italian war. Gnaeus Pompey was prosecuted on charges of having helped himself illegally to spoils from Asculum after its capture in the Italian war, though it is probable that the real charge against him was that of being the son of Pompeius Strabo, who had led his army against the Marians. The failure of this prosecution signalled that Cinna had no intention of prolonging the witch hunt for Sullan supporters. Metellus Pius had taken refuge in Africa, and he was allowed to remain there in peace though a decree of exile was probably passed against him.

There are signs that a reconciliation with Sulla's supporters was attempted. Marius had executed Lucius Caesar, but his close relative Caius Julius Caesar – the future triumvir and dictator – was promoted to the chief priesthood in Rome, the office of *flamen dialis*, and linked by marriage to Cinna. Philippus, one of the chief opponents of Livius Drusus, was made censor in 86 BC (and on Philippus' watch the Sulpician promise to distribute the new Italian citizens evenly through all the tribes was quietly dropped.) It was evidently clear to Cinna and the senate that eventually something was going to have to be done about Sulla, but while there was a chance of a negotiated outcome there was little point in inflaming the situation further.

Sulla later claimed that Fimbria's army had been sent out to the east in order to defeat him, but this is probably later propaganda. For a long while this senatorial army and the army of Sulla campaigned against Mithridates, if not together then at least without seriously interfering with each other.

Likewise, both Sulla and a senate-appointed general claim to have campaigned against opportunist tribal raiders in Macedonia, but there are no reports of clashes between the two Roman factions. In fact we know from two separate sources[1] that Sulla and the senate were agreed that dealing with Mithridates came before internal political disagreements. The problem came in 85 BC when it became clear that Mithridates was, if not down and out, at least on the ropes. The senatorial army of Fimbria succeeded in bottling Mithridates up in the port of Pitane in Asia Minor. Escape by sea was blocked by a fleet commanded by Sulla's loyal subordinate Lucullus,[2] so it appeared that the capture of the enemy king was inevitable.

Sulla had different plans. He was already negotiating with Mithridates to bring the war to an end. There was no guarantee that the war would end with the capture of the king, but negotiations certainly would end, leaving Sulla to start negotiating again from the beginning with whomever took over from Mithridates in Pontus. This was unacceptable, as Sulla wanted the war done with so that he could get back to pressing matters waiting for him in Italy. As the campaigning season drew to a close, Sulla and Mithridates made a deal. Mithridates would give up all the conquests that the Romans had not taken back from him already, and he would make reparation with ships, money and supplies for the massacre of Romans and Italians perpetrated on his orders. Sulla intended that the cities of Asia Minor that had done the actual massacring would also pay in due course, but for the moment Mithridates' penance gave his army a handy fill-up of money and resources for the coming campaign in Italy.

The outbreak of peace in Asia Minor left the senatorial army of Fimbria's men with the choice of either fighting Sulla or joining him. They chose to join, though from the army's later performance it is clear that they chose Sulla less from enthusiasm than as the lesser of two evils. Sulla had nothing against Fimbria and even offered to allow the now unemployed general to sail back to Rome, but Fimbria opted for suicide instead. After all, he had killed a serving consul to take command of his army, so his reception in Rome would have been problematic at best.

Sulla now wrote to the senate:

In a high-handed manner he recounted his deeds while still a mere quaestor in Africa during the war against Jugurtha, his services in the Cimbric war, as praetor in Cilicia, and in the Italian war and as consul. … He made the most of relating how those banished from Rome by Cinna had fled to him and had received his help and support in their distress.[3] Yet he [Sulla] had been declared a public enemy, his house had been destroyed, his friends executed and his wife and children forced to flee for their lives. On his return he would take revenge for this on all those in the city who were guilty, but all others, including the new citizens, had nothing to fear from him.

Appian BC 1.77

It is uncertain how the senate were expected to receive this missive. Quite possibly Sulla intended it in the spirit that the senate received it – as the opening position in a round of negotiation. The senate's reply was in kind. They acknowledged Sulla's service to his country both previously and in the defeat of Mithridates, and they ostentatiously ordered Cinna not to raise troops against Sulla. The senate also urged Sulla to respond at once to their overtures, and assured him that they would guarantee his security in the meantime. Sulla would undoubtedly have noted the implicit gambit that if the senate had to guarantee his security this would be because he was no longer a proconsul in charge of an army. Thus, in diplomatic language Sulla was invited to lay down his arms and throw himself at the mercy of the senate. The two sides were far apart, but at least they were talking. Optimists must have hoped that a further round of bloodshed could be averted.

Cinna entered in the spirit of the thing. Appian claims that he panicked, disregarded the senatorial instruction and immediately began mustering an army. This is unlikely, though Cinna must have been aware that Sulla's intentions for him were far from benign. Cinna did indeed begin mustering an army, yet the interesting thing is that he began mustering it on the eastern seaboard of Italy at Ancona.[4] As the modern historian Badian has convincingly argued,[5] the reason for mustering an army at this port could be neither to defend Italy nor, as some have claimed, to launch a pre-emptive invasion of Greece. An army at Ancona could only cross east to one point – Liburnia on the Balkan coast. The Liburnians were notorious pirates and it is highly improbable they had not been taking advantage of the recent crisis to plunder merchant shipping to their heart's content. So Cinna would raise an army and take it to Liburnia to punish the pirates. Sulla could not complain about a Roman consul conducting standard military operations while negotiations went on, even though such operations would also leave Cinna with an experienced army under his command should negotiations fail. But failure was not inevitable. Sulla's next reply went a long way towards meeting the senate's implicit demand. All he claimed to want was to be restored to Rome, along with those who had fled to exile with him. The rest he would leave to the senate.

At this point fate intervened. It was now early in 84 BC – in fact too early for a safe sea crossing to Illyria, but Cinna was in a hurry. He needed to get his army trained and experienced by the time Sulla brought his veterans back from Asia. This Sulla certainly would do, because even if the political issues were peacefully resolved, these men had fought their war and were due to be disbanded. If Sulla's negotiations with the senate went well, his soldiers could justifiably expect to celebrate a triumph in Rome for their hard-fought victories in Greece. If negotiations went badly, these men could expect to do further fighting in Italy. Cinna knew this, and his men did too. They felt, reasonably enough, that Cinna was risking their lives on a rough ocean crossing to take them to fight an unnecessary war, which left their homes at risk should Sulla return before they were disentangled from the campaign over the Adriatic. Cinna did what he could to restore order with his disgruntled army. He called the striking soldiery to an assembly in which he misjudged the mood of his men. It should be remembered that Roman armies had recently, on two separate occasions lynched commanders who were not to their liking. Perhaps Cinna felt that as a consul of Rome his men would not dare to do the same to him. He was wrong. A tussle between one of his attendants and an obstreperous soldier quickly developed into a full-scale riot in which Cinna was killed. With Marius already dead, Rome had now lost two serving consuls, and with Cinna went the last decent chance of a peaceful resolution to the crisis.

Gnaeus Carbo, the consul who had replaced Marius, was unable to maintain order. Carbo quickly fell out with the senate, which insisted on him coming to Rome for the election of a replacement for Cinna. For whatever reason, Carbo was reluctant to do so and only turned up when forced by the threat that the tribunes would rescind his own powers. Even when they had got their consul to Rome, the senate found that getting him a colleague was not easy. Carbo and his supporters consistently found unfavourable omens that prevented the elections from taking place. Eventually the attempt was abandoned and Carbo remained sole consul for the rest of the year.

In a further attempt to speed up negotiations with Sulla, the senate decreed that all armies should be disbanded, a move intended not so much to make Sulla's army illegal than as a response to Carbo who was busily building up an army of his own. Resentment at government recruiting efforts in Picenum meant that no troops were recruited there until later when the young Pompey exploited that resentment to gather his own private army. In Africa Metellus Pius declared his support for Sulla and apparently tried to bring over the province to that cause, but the governor had been expecting this, and Metellus was easily thwarted.

Nevertheless, the government was at odds with itself; there was unrest in the provinces, private armies springing up and a consul had been murdered by his own men. No matter that the root cause of most of this disruption was Sulla himself. That Rome was in a parlous state was all the justification that Sulla needed to take matters into his own hands. As he had done in 88 BC in his earlier march on Rome, now in the spring of 83 BC Sulla set out for Italy publicly announcing his intention of 'restoring order'.

A letter sent ahead to the senate said that Sulla had no intention of being reconciled with his enemies; however, if the senate insisted, he would spare their lives. Furthermore, Sulla would protect the senate, including those members of that body who had been driven to take refuge with him in Greece. This offer to protect the senate neatly reversed the senate's offer to protect Sulla, and amounted to a rejection of the senate's earlier proposal. Sulla himself would not need protection because he could rely on the loyalty of his troops – which meant that any suggestion that Sulla would disband his men was now off the negotiating table. This did not mean that talks had broken down, but with Cinna's death and the subsequent outbreak of disorder, Sulla's position was stronger and his negotiating position had changed to reflect this.

The consuls for the next year were L. Scipio Asiaticus and C. Norbanus. The pair were less sanguine than the senate about a negotiated settlement, but in any case, as the executive officers of the state, it was their job to prepare for the worst should things come to that. The former consul, Carbo took command of the province of Cisalpine Gaul. This secured the north for the government and left the new consuls to manage the defence of the south. War was still not inevitable. No attempt was made to prevent Sulla returning to Italy and he landed unopposed at Brundisium. Technically speaking, this was not an invasion but merely an ex-consul returning with his army from a successful foreign war. This was as it should be, but the omens were dire. Literally so; there were earthquakes, the temple of Jupiter on the Capitoline hill was destroyed in a fire, and strange events were reported, such as a woman in Etruria who gave birth to a live snake.[6]

Sulla crossed to Campania where matters came to the crunch, for the consul Norbanus moved to block the progress of Sulla's army with one of his own. Until now, Sulla had been an obstreperous ex-consul who had taken some legally dubious actions. Anyway, the killing of Octavius and the persecution of Sulla's friends, not to mention the excesses of Marius before his death, all meant that the government could hardly claim the moral, legal or constitutional high ground. Ideally, it would be best if the events of the past decade could be, if not forgotten, at least left in disreputable obscurity. Sulla later claimed to have hoped for as much – it is almost certainly from his memoirs that we get the report that Norbanus arrested the envoys sent by Sulla for last-minute negotiations, and instead prepared for battle. It may be that Norbanus rejected this last chance for peace because he fancied his prospects against an army of around 10–12,000 men, which is all Sulla is said to have had with him at the time.

So the next round of Rome's civil wars formally resumed somewhere around Canusium, or possibly at the crossing of the River Volturnus where Norbanus took the chance of crushing the Sullan threat for once and for all. He quickly discovered that a well-generalled veteran army coming off a hard campaign can punch well above its weight. Despite its superior numbers the government army was soundly defeated, and the remnants fled to Capua, which had recently been made a Roman colony in an effort by the government to secure the city's loyalty. Norbanus camped at Mt Tifana about a mile from Capua's walls and there awaited the arrival of L. Scipio, his fellow-consul. When Scipio turned up with his army, Sulla immediately attempted to open negotiations with the new arrival. This may be an example of Sulla being reasonable, or it may simply indicate opportunism on Sulla's part. Sulla knew that the loyalty of his own army had been forged and tested in the first march on Rome and in the Mithridatic wars that had followed. He also knew that Scipio's army had no such personal bond with its commander. Furthermore, Scipio's men were deeply uncomfortable about fighting Sulla's men, partly because they did not really want to fight fellow Romans, and partly because they had a well-founded suspicion that those fellow Romans would comprehensively defeat them if they tried. Therefore, should he reject Sulla's overtures Scipio would be cast in the role of the aggressor, the man who wanted death and bloodshed despite the best efforts of Sulla, and the earnest wish of his own men.

Matters were further complicated by Sertorius, who was becoming thoroughly frustrated with how his superior officers were conducting the war. It was very clear to Sertorius that Sulla was playing the peacemaker in order to subvert Scipio's army. Scipio himself appears to have had hopes that the negotiations would actually lead somewhere, so he sent a messenger to Norbanus to hold off hostilities while talks were in progress. That messenger was Sertorius, who while *en route* to Norbanus' camp deliberately broke the ceasefire (and incidentally secured the army's line of retreat) by capturing the town of Suessa from Sulla. Scipio was taken aback by this unilateral move, and by way of apology released the hostages Sulla had given as an earnest of his good faith. However, the damage was done. Scipio's army was outraged at thus being committed to a battle it did not want and every man defected to Sulla. Appian tells us, 'Scipio and his son were left alone in their tent, themselves the last remnant of their entire army. While they were wondering what to do, Sulla came up and captured them.'[7]

With Scipio and his army painlessly removed from the war, the government side was now represented by Norbanus and Marius, the son of the deceased Marius.[8] The government used the younger Marius heavily in their propaganda, relying on the fondness the common people still felt for the father. The promotion and honours for a man who had done little to merit them (apart from his choice of parent) was something else that infuriated the more deserving and capable Sertorius. Since the débâcle at Suessa, Sertorius and the rest of the government leaders were no longer on speaking terms, so Sertorius took himself out of the war in Italy and went – or was kicked – to Iberia;[9] which is another reason why only Norbanus and Marius (jnr) were left to fight Sulla. The government forces had a strong position, for Mt Tifana commands the approaches to Capua. For this reason there had been a major battle 200 years previously at the same location when the Campanians had dug in on the mountain to defend the city from advancing Samnites.

Always on the lookout for ways to increase morale, Sulla claimed that an apparition of two goats fighting in the sky was a favourable omen, thus using what may have simply been a fortuitous combination of cloud shapes to get his men speedily into position. Norbanus probably expected a more cautious approach, and the sudden arrival of the enemy caught his army in mid-deployment. Sulla and his experienced men immediately seized the moment and fell upon the government army without breaking stride for the usual pre-battle preliminaries. The fight was short and nasty, with 7,000 men killed on the government side for few casualties among their veteran opponents. Norbanus had suffered his second defeat of the war, and he now retreated into Capua itself, and all that prevented Sulla from advancing on Rome was the early arrival of what was to prove an unusually severe winter.

Mt Tifana and its prelude at Canusium was not the only military action of 83 BC, because Sulla now had allies. As mentioned above, Pompey had raised himself a tidy little army of three legions in Picenum. With these he set out to join Sulla. On the way he was confronted by three government detachments, which deployed to surround him. Nothing daunted, Pompey assembled his army into a compact formation and routed that detachment immediately before him. This caused consternation among the government commanders who failed to agree on what to do next. In the end, they marched off and left Pompey alone, not least because large numbers of their men were enthusiastically defecting to Pompey's side. Soon afterwards, at the river Arsis on the border with Umbria, Pompey received a useful reinforcement of cavalry. This had been sent against him by Carbo. Showing off the skills he had picked up from his father in the Italian war, Pompey manoeuvred this cavalry on to unfavourable ground where unable to fight or flee, the horsemen surrendered and joined the Sullan side.[10] When Pompey finally joined Sulla, the latter ordered his army's standards to be lowered. This was the customary salute of a Roman commander to a fellow general, even though no one had promoted Pompey to his command but Pompey himself.

Other areas also fell to Sullan supporters. After his misadventures in Africa, Metellus Pius had moved to Liguria in the far north-west of the Italian peninsula. There he started raising troops for Sulla. L. Philippus, the former censor and veteran opponent of Livius Drusus, now reverted to his conservative roots by declaring for Sulla, taking with him the province of Sardinia, which he had been sent to hold for the government. However, the most significant military action in the north was fought by Lucullus, the brother of the officer who had been with Sulla from the beginning. At Fidentia (modern Fidenza) he took on fifty enemy cohorts with just sixteen of his own, and won, mainly due to the superior morale of his troops.[11]

Thus, by the time winter brought campaigning to an end in 83 BC Sulla now controlled Liguria, Sardinia and isolated areas of northern Italy, and also had Picenum, Apulia and most of Campania – with the exception of Capua where Norbanus remained stubbornly behind the walls rejecting every overture of peace. The reaction of the Italians to Sulla's arrival would be crucial to success or failure in 82 BC, so Sulla spent much of the winter in diplomatic overtures to Rome's newest citizens. He had already made a start by insisting on rigid discipline among his men, who were firmly instructed to treat the Italian countryside as friendly territory. There was no looting or pillage and anything the army took was paid for. (Another advantage of the huge fines levied on Mithridates and the cities of Asia minor was that Sulla and his men could afford to do this.) Now Sulla went further, and announced that whatever the government had offered the Italians, he would honour – which meant that the Italians were finally evenly distributed through the voting tribes, as they had always demanded. Only one Italian faction failed to be convinced. The Samnites and Lucanians had been pretty much left to their own devices by a Roman government, which considered it had enough on its plate without unnecessarily provoking some of the best fighters in Italy. These mountain tribes saw Sulla as a threat, and they allied with the government armies in a fervent effort to keep the *de facto* independence they had enjoyed for most of the previous decade.

In Rome itself, positions hardened. Sulla's undisguised intention to take control of the city focussed the minds of those who had joined with Marius in persecuting Sulla's friends. Sulla tried to show moderation by releasing Scipio unharmed, but for 82 BC the people nevertheless elected as consuls two hard-liners to continue the struggle. These were C. Carbo (again) and the completely unqualified son of Marius. Sulla's feud with Marius was thus set to continue into the next generation. The younger Marius decided to personally take on the job of containing Sulla at the start of the campaigning season, which began in an ill-omened spring marred by frequent and heavy rains. Despite the weather, Sulla took the offensive and began a march up the Via Latina in order to join reinforcements under Dolabella, another aristocrat who had defected to him. His army was shadowed on the way north by that of the younger Marius who was, in the best family tradition, reluctant to offer battle until he caught his enemy in a vulnerable position. Sulla in his turn was eager for battle because he was a strong believer in omens, and had been informed by a soothsayer that this was the best time to fight. Since he wanted his forces to be combined with those of Dolabella before any battle began, Sulla pushed his men hard despite the unfavourable marching conditions. Even if not aware of Sulla's date with destiny, the younger Marius knew that it would be a good idea to keep Sulla and Dolabella apart for as long as possible, so his skirmishers worked hard to slow Sulla up – a task made easier by the weather and terrain.

Sulla's push forward ended at a place called Sacriportus, somewhere in the upper valley of the River Trerus (the modern Sacco) near where the city of Fregellae had once stood (p.18). At this point Sulla's officers showed him some of the men collapsed on their shields through sheer exhaustion. Sulla was forced to concede that his army could go no further and gave orders to make camp. It seemed that the younger Marius had finally got his enemy where he wanted him. Sulla's army was dog-tired and seemed demoralized after a day spent grappling with Marian skirmishers. Just to let their enemies get even more exhausted, the Marians waited until their opponents had spent more energy digging the standard ditch that usually surrounds a Roman marching camp. Then, as the Sullan army started work on the camp ramparts, the Marians attacked. There are reports that say that the younger Marius was as exhausted as the Sullans by the day's events and was already asleep by the time the attack took place. Yet others allege that the younger Marius was at the head of his army, riding before the lines to encourage the men.[12] These contrary reports illustrate the difficulties faced by historians studying this period, both now and later in antiquity. Not only are sources scarce, but so partisan that it is sometimes possible to tell from the bias whether a later writer such as Plutarch is drawing from an anti-Sullan source or from the writings of one of Sulla's supporters. Certainly one of the most influential sources in antiquity is – and was intended so to be from the start – the *Memoirs* of Sulla himself.

It is probably from the latter source that we discover that Sulla's men were not demoralized, as the Marians believed, but instead frustrated by their inability to get to grips with their enemy. So when the source of that frustration attacked them directly, the Sullans gladly downed their entrenching tools in exchange for swords. Not having had time to build a rampart, the men simply inserted their heavy throwing spears ['pilums'] into the earth to form a makeshift palisade and swiftly organizing themselves behind this, they went directly at the enemy with swords. Again the progress of the actual battle depends on which source one believes. The historian Plutarch reports that 'the enemy did not hold their ground for long before they fled' – and this report is given greater credibility by the fact that throughout the war Marian morale was always fragile, with soldiers ready to either flee from or surrender to the more determined and experienced Sullan army. However, by other accounts[13] the army fought stubbornly. This is also possible, for the Marian ranks now included a goodly contingent of Samnites and Lucanians, and these men were a match for anybody. However, the greater experience of the Sullan army told, and either speedily or slowly the Marian left began to buckle. That was all the signal needed for five cohorts of Marian infantry and some of the cavalry to change sides and go over to the Sullan army. This in turn caused a general collapse, and the Marian army scattered in rout.

Sulla's men proved that the stimulus of an unexpected victory was a sovereign cure for fatigue, for they and their general followed up the beaten enemy mercilessly and hounded the beaten army through the countryside.

Sulla himself reports that his army killed 20,000 men and captured another 8,000 (a figure that may include the 5,000 who deserted to him in mid-battle), while he himself lost only twenty-three men. This latter figure is either suspect or proof that Sulla's soldiers were exceptionally good at caring for themselves – Sulla gives a similarly light casualty toll for his army in 86 BC after the battle of Chaeronea against the Pontic army in Greece. In this case, the pursuit of the beaten Marians took the Sullan army right to the walls of the city of Praeneste, just 35km (22 miles) from Rome. As often happened in these situations, the city's defenders were reluctant to hold open the gates for the fleeing army because their foes were pressing so close on their heels that it would prove impossible to close the gates against a torrent of men, and the city itself would be captured. So the gates were closed in the face of the Marian refugees, leading to many being slaughtered directly beneath the walls. Ropes were flung down so that individuals could be pulled up to the ramparts, and this is how the younger Marius eventually escaped. However, he was now bottled up in Praeneste, and the Marian army in the south was effectively destroyed.

Things were not going much better for the Marians in the north. Metellus and Pompey had an effective rivalry going, whereby a success by one general spurred the other to greater efforts. In his efforts to hold northern Italy, Carbo had made his base at Arimimum (Rimini) and from there sent his generals Carrinas and Censorinus against their Sullan counterparts. Metellus defeated Carrinas on the northern borders of Picenum, not far from Pompey's earlier victory at the river Aesis, and Pompey himself went on to take Sena Gallica and then brutally sacked the town. Carbo decided to take the field personally, but was checked by the news of the defeat of the younger Marius at Sacriportus. By now Norbanus had escaped from Capua, so Carbo handed over command of the northern army to the former consul and headed south to see what could be retrieved of the situation there. The younger Marius decided that his personal situation was probably irretrievable and, again in the best family tradition, was determined to at least take personal revenge on his enemies no matter how detrimental this was to the state.

He wrote to Brutus, the city Praetor and told him to invent some pretext or the other for summoning the senate. There he was to kill Publius Antistius [the father-in-law of Pompey] and the other Papirius [the original being Carbo himself], Lucius Domitius and the Pontifex Maximus, Mucius Scaevola. Assassins brought into the senate house for this purpose killed the first two of these men in their seats as arranged. Domitius made a run for it but was killed at the door while Scaevola did not manage to get much further. Their bodies were thrown into the Tiber, for it was by now the custom not to bury those so killed.

Appian BC 1.88

This is what it had come to – senators, even the Pontifex Maximus himself – being assassinated in the senate house on a consul's orders. Many senators who witnessed the occasion would have been present just under a decade previously. At that time the senate house had rejected the legislation of Livius Drusus, legislation that might well have prevented the entire sordid tragedy before it got started. For many years a shrine to victory had existed in the senate house. On that day a shrine to Nemesis would have been more appropriate, as the senate continued to suffer the bitter consequences of its pride and folly in 91 BC. Drusus had predicted that the senate would pay – the senate was paying now, and still the full price had not been met.

Most of southern Italy now belonged to Sulla, though some cities such as Praeneste remained under siege. The Sullan faction tended to be brutal toward such places when they were captured so as to strike fear into other towns contemplating resistance further north. Neapolis (Naples) fell to the Sullans through treachery, and virtually the entire population was massacred. Consequently, Appian remarks that towns near Rome promptly surrendered to the Sullans 'with fear and trembling; at Ostia the city opened its gates to them'.[14] The war moved north into Etruria, where armies led by Sulla and Carbo clashed directly. Sulla was successful in a minor cavalry action against Celtiberian cavalry sent from Hispania to reinforce the Marian army. This led to a few hundred of these men deserting to Sulla, whereupon Carbo executed those who had remained loyal. Though a minor incident in itself, this demonstrates Carbo's extreme frustration with the constant flow of desertions from his army to the Sullan side. The punishment was itself counter-productive, in that units still deserted, but they now tended to leave no one behind to face their commander's wrath.

Further north, things were going no better for Norbanus than they had for Carbo when he commanded there. M. Lucullus was besieged at Placentia, but broke the siege and scattered his opponents with a successful sortie from behind the walls. Thereafter Norbanus attempted to get the better of Metellus by a forced march, only to have his Sullan opponent fall on his exhausted army at the end of it, and destroy all but a thousand men. In Etruria Sulla and Carbo fought an indecisive all-day action against each other somewhere near the town of Clusium. Though Carbo thereby succeeded in checking Sulla's northward advance, it appears he achieved this by pulling manpower from other government forces operating in the north. Certainly his other generals had a rough time of it, and lack of manpower could not have helped. Pompey and Crassus were working together at this point (as they would later do when, together with Julius Caesar, they dominated Rome as the so called 'first triumvirate'). Carbo's general Carrinas was severely defeated by the pair, losing some 3,000 men. After the battle Carrinas took refuge in the nearby town of Spoletium and called on Carbo for help. As the steady flow of defections to his side demonstrates, Sulla had a large number of sympathizers within the enemy camp. With advance intelligence of the enemy's intentions, he set up an ambush for the reinforcing troops and killed a further 2,000 when he caught them unawares on the march. Carrinas thereafter took advantage of the vile spring weather to escape while heavy rain cloaked his movements.

Good intelligence and poor Marian morale also led to the downfall of an attempt to relieve Marius at Praeneste. Eight legions were sent by Carbo to break the siege, but Pompey was waiting. The Marians were again ambushed, and though their commander managed to extract much of the army intact, the morale of the men took a heavy blow. One legion simply abandoned its commander and took itself back to Ariminum while most of the rest quietly deserted and went home. Just seven cohorts returned to Carbo, leaving Praeneste unrelieved and increasingly suffering from hunger. Each defeat suffered by the Marians had a knock-on effect leading to other setbacks as both officers and men saw their cause as increasingly hopeless.

One Albinovanus was the leader of a Lucanian legion that defected to Sulla. To prove that he personally was loyal, Albinovanus invited Norbanus and his senior officers to a banquet. Norbanus was unable to attend the feast but his senior officers attended. In the course of the meal, as he had previously arranged with Sulla, Albinovanus put his guests to death. This in turn led to the revolt of Ariminum to the Sullan side. With the loss of his senior officers to treachery, Norbanus had now had enough. Like many of the men fighting on his side, he no longer believed that the war could be won, so he abandoned his army and fled to the east. He later committed suicide in Rhodes, very publicly in the market-place as a reproach to the citizens who were debating whether to hand him over to Sulla. Carbo soon followed his colleague's example. He had tried and failed yet again to break through to Praeneste with two legions, and this final failure combined with Norbanus' defection finally broke his will. Though he still had large forces available to him in Etruria, he had lost faith in the Marian cause, and he also fled, in his case to Africa.

This meant that the Sullans were now dominant in north Italy, Campania, Apulia and much of the south. The only unfinished business appeared to be the Marian army in Etruria, which now lacked a leader, and the younger Marius in Praeneste, who lacked an army. However, what was good news for the Sullan cause was terrible news for the Samnites, who realized that once Sulla had secured Rome, the reconquest of their territory would be his next item of business. And as Sulla had already given earnest of his intentions by executing such Samnite prisoners as he captured, the Samnites justifiably feared that the Roman reconquest of their homeland would be a brutal and bloody affair. So the current civil war and the last remnants of the Italian war now combined into a final convulsion, which was to determine the fate of Rome. In the absence of Carbo and Norbanus, the Samnite leader Pontius Telesinus became by default the leader of the anti-Sullan cause. By rallying his own people and gathering allies from wherever possible in southern Italy, he raised an army of 70,000 men. If these were the scrapings of the bottom of the anti-Sullan barrel it should be remembered that they were from a very formidable barrel indeed. Many of the men in Telesinus' army were veterans who had repeatedly defeated the Roman legions in the war of 90 BC and were ready, willing and able to do so again.

The first task facing Telesinus was to unite the army in Etruria with the younger Marius in Praeneste, since while Telesinus was sure of the loyalty of his own men, he was an unlikely representative of what was still the government of Rome. To command non-Samnite troops such as those abandoned by Carbo, he needed a Roman consul, and to get that Roman consul he had to lift the siege of Praeneste. That was no easy undertaking, because the Sullans entrusted with the siege of that city had spent their time raising a massive series of earthworks, which stretched deep into the Alban hills. Praeneste was very defensible, but the very factors that made it hard to attack also made it hard for relief troops to get near – especially since Sulla, currently with no other pressing business on hand, had put himself and his army squarely across Telesinus' route. The younger Marius tried to play his part and sallied from the walls and established a large fort close to the Roman siege lines, but his effort was in vain. Even Telesinus and his Samnites were not prepared to push the issue against Sulla once his veteran army had dug itself into a secure position. The siege of Praeneste continued.

Meanwhile Norbanus' generals, Censorinus and Carrinas, driven from the north, now took control of whatever remained of the forces abandoned by Carbo in Etruria. These attempted to join up with Telesinus to form the last, but very formidable, Marian army in Italy.

Matters were now coming to a head. Sulla and his army braced themselves for a final desperate attempt by the enemy to break through the siege lines and relieve Praeneste – but this did not happen. Telesinus realized that Praeneste was a trap. He had Sulla dug in before him, and Crassus and another army closing in from behind. Being a highly experienced soldier, he swiftly changed objectives, broke camp by night and unexpectedly marched on Rome.

The prize of the war, the city of Rome itself, had been largely untouched by the conflict thus far. After the battle of Sacriportus had broken the government army in the south and led to Marius being penned up in Praeneste, Rome had been virtually defenceless. Appian[15] reports that Sulla had briefly visited the city on the way north to engage with Carbo in Etruria. On arriving in Rome Sulla discovered that the Marian government officials had fled, so he called an assembly of the people and assured them that they had nothing to fear from him. He then appointed men to continue the essential functions of city administration and rushed off northward to re-engage with his enemies. By the rules of war, Sulla's brief stopover and appointment of officials meant that from the Marian perspective, Rome was now an enemy city. From the Samnite perspective of course, Rome had seldom been anything but. Now, because Sulla and his subordinates had done a good job of preventing the northern Marians under Carrinas and Censorinus from uniting their troops with the Samnite army, the force marching toward Rome was largely composed of Samnites and others who bore the city nothing but ill-will.

It is true that Rome had little strategic value at this time, but in another sense it was what the war was all about. To use a more modern analogy, it was as though, in a game of chess Telesinus had been working to aid his embattled queen when he had suddenly switched tactics and attacked his opponent's king. The Samnites were well aware that a Sullan victory would see their lands devastated and their cities sacked by a vindictive Roman army. By hitting Rome, Telesinus was offering his men a chance to get their retaliation in first. However, there was also a cool, rational aspect to his planning – with the Samnites in their present mood, there was no way that Sulla could hold station before Praeneste and let the enemy have their way with the city he claimed to represent. Tactically, he should remain where he was, keeping the enemy armies apart and maintaining the siege of Praeneste. Politically, Telesinus had forced his hand. Sulla was compelled to abandon his carefully dug earthworks and make a forced march to defend Rome.

This is not to say that Sulla was unhappy that Telesinus had brought things to the crunch. Sulla had an unwavering faith in his own destiny and an equal faith in the army he commanded. Throughout the Mithridatic wars that had forged his army into the superb fighting force that it currently was, Sulla had sought to engage with the enemy at the earliest opportunity. However, in all his major battles to date Sulla had generally been able to prepare deployments and even earthworks in advance. This time he was going in blind against an enemy who was ready and waiting for him. Nevertheless, offered the opportunity to bring a decade of warfare to an end, Sulla unhesitatingly took that opportunity and followed the Samnites on their night march to Rome.

At daybreak, the appearance of the a hostile army just over a mile from Rome caused consternation in the city. 'Naturally there was tumult, with women shrieking and people running back and forth as though the city had already been taken' remarks Plutarch.[16] A scion of one of Rome's noblest families, Appius Claudius, joined a force of cavalry who rode out to delay the attackers. Those watching from the ramparts were appalled to see their war-hardened opponents swiftly and professionally chop the impromptu Roman force – and Appius Claudius – to pieces. However the delay did allow seven hundred horsemen sent ahead by Sulla to catch their breath, organize and begin harassing the Samnite army. Seven hundred cavalry could do little against an army that outnumbered them a hundred to one, but their presence signalled to those in Rome that Sulla was aware of the situation, and was on his way. This stiffened Roman spines and prevented any premature surrender and it also stopped Telesinus from doing anything premature. Even if storming the lightly defended walls of Rome would be little more than a formality, the Samnite army would hardly want Sulla turning up at their backs while they were doing so. Therefore Telesinus deployed his forces slightly away from the Colline Gate (literally the 'Hill Gate') to the north-east of the city, and waited for Sulla to arrive.

For Sulla, the choice of battlefield was fortuitous. Sulla claimed to be the protégé of Venus, and her temple of Venus Erycina was within sight of the gate, and the other major temple in the vicinity was to Fortuna, the goddess on whom Sulla had relied all his career. And indeed, when Sulla arrived with his main army at around noon, the temple of Venus was where he took his stand.

> This was the critical moment, and not just for Sulla. Since Hannibal had made his camp within the third milestone [from Rome] the city had faced no greater danger than when Telesinus went from rank to rank of his army saying 'Now the Romans face their last day.' Loudly he exhorted his army to defeat the Romans and destroy their city saying 'These are the wolves who have been tearing at the liberty of Italy. They will never go away until we have cut down the wood that shelters them.'
>
> Velleius Paterculus, *History* 2.27.

Sulla's commanders were concerned by the state of the troops after their rapid overnight march as they attempted to catch up with the Samnites. The officers pointed out that they were not up against the generally demoralized and disorganized soldiers of Carbo or Marius, but Samnites and Lucanians – highly motivated, experienced and warlike opponents. They urged Sulla to wait, at least overnight. But Sulla had faith in Fortuna, and only allowed his men a few hours to rest and take a meal. Then he organized his battle lines, and at four o'clock that November afternoon, with the sun already sinking, the final battle of the Italian and civil war was begun. As might be expected given the high quality of the troops involved, the battle was a close and desperate affair. Sulla's legionaries were arguably the best soldiers in the world at that time, but they had marched all night, and were outnumbered by an enemy almost as good as they were.

The Roman left wing began to buckle. Sulla's men were forced backward until they literally had their backs to the wall – that being the wall of Rome beside the Colline gate. Those in the rearmost ranks began to seek shelter within the city, but the veterans manning the walls were having none of it. They dropped the portcullis on the men streaming in, killing not a few and forcing the rest to turn and fight. Sulla realized the situation was desperate and rushed to the scene on his distinctive white horse. So distinctive was this horse that even the enemy recognized it. Two advantageously positioned javelineers took advantage of Sulla's distraction and attempted to impale the Roman commander with a pair of well-flung spears. Sulla was unaware of his doom sailing through the air until the groom riding alongside desperately slashed Sulla's white horse across the rump. The startled animal leapt forward, losing a few hairs of its tail to the spears which flew behind Sulla's back as he rushed unharmed into the ranks of his fragmenting army. In vain Sulla pleaded with his men, threatened some and even physically laid hands on others to turn them back to face the enemy.

> There is a story that Sulla had a little golden image of Apollo from Delphi which he always carried with him in battle. Now he took it out and kissed it affectionately saying 'Apollo, in so many struggles you have raised Sulla the Fortunate to glory and greatness. Did you do it just to bring him here, to the gates of his native city where he and his fellow-countrymen are to be cast down to a shameful death?'
>
> Plutarch, *Life of Sulla* 29

It certainly looked that way, for Sulla's efforts were in vain. The ranks he was trying to keep in place were completely shattered with heavy casualties. Sulla ended up back in his camp with one group of fugitives, while others fled to the detachment still keeping guard on Praeneste to tell the commander there that the battle was lost. As Plutarch remarks (ibid.) 'It looked as though it was all over.'

That was when messengers arrived from Crassus, who had taken command of the right wing with his army while Sulla gave his full attention to the left. Crassus reported that his men had totally defeated the enemy facing them and chased them back past the town of Antemnae two miles down the Via Salaria. Crassus wanted to know if he could have supplies so that his men could now break for supper. This, to put it mildly, put a new perspective on things. Instead of Sulla commanding a broken army on the brink of total defeat, the battle was currently a fifty-fifty draw. In fact the situation was even somewhat better than that, because the morale of Sulla's remaining men soared on the news that the battle was not yet lost, while the Samnites facing them were dejected to discover that despite their efforts the battle was not yet won. Furthermore, Crassus was bringing to the second instalment of the battle men who had beaten their enemy once and were therefore more confident of being able to do so again.

Whether these men got their well-deserved supper before returning to action is unknown. In fact, not much other information survives of the battle thereafter, apart from some reports that it went on all night. It must have been a grim affair, with two armies of veteran soldiers who knew that they were fighting not just for themselves but the survival of their homeland. As a night action, the fighting was confused and the commanders on each side could do little in the way of tactical manoeuvre. It was down to the men themselves fighting sword-on-sword in a bitter, drawn-out conflict. It was afterwards estimated that some 50,000 men lost their lives in that one battle.[17] Some time before dawn Telesinus was mortally wounded, and a Roman surge captured the Samnite camp. It became clear that the Romans were going to emerge with a hard-won victory, and the Samnite force divided itself into those slain, those fled and those taken prisoner – the latter, by varying accounts between 6,000 and 8,000 in number.

Essentially this battle ended the wars, both civil and Italian. Sulla's victory broke the Samnites and Lucanians – the last bastion of Italian resistance – and demoralized the army of Carrinas and Censorinus. On news of the defeat of their cause, both Marian generals attempted to emulate the example of Carbo and Norbanus and flee abroad, but they had left it too late. They were quickly captured and brought to Sulla. Sulla had nothing personal against these two men, who had fought on behalf of a legitimately elected Roman government and had supported their cause to the last. Nevertheless, Sulla intended that these men should now serve his purposes and that they would do so better dead than alive. Both men were killed without trial, because Sulla wanted their heads. These heads and that of Telesinus (the latter with his dying expression 'more like a conqueror than a beaten man'[18])were displayed on spears to Marius at Praeneste to make it abundantly clear to him that all hope was lost.

There are conflicting accounts as to what happened to Marius thereafter. The Sullan tradition is that Marius attempted to escape like a rat through tunnels carefully dug for that purpose. However, the exits to the tunnels had been discovered long before, and Marius popped up only to be cut down again by guards stationed for that purpose. In the alternative tradition, once they saw that escape was impossible, Marius and the younger brother of Telesinus agreed on a sort of mutual murder pact. Each rushed at the other with a drawn sword and was stabbed through. So perished the last of Sulla's enemies, a man, as one historian puts it 'not unworthy of his father'.

Chapter 10

Terror and Settlement

With his victory at the Colline Gate, Sulla had finally overcome all opposition. As with Mithridates before them, the Samnites and Marians had fallen to Sulla's veteran legionaries. Soon after the final battle, the senate was summoned to meet its new master at the temple of Bellona. This venue may have struck some as a positive sign. The Roman senate was a body of men rather than a place, and could legally assemble in any temple (in fact, technically speaking, the senate house was a temple of Victory). However, the important thing about the temple of Bellona was that the Roman war-goddess was domiciled outside the official boundary of Rome. Sulla was a proconsul returning with an army, and he was therefore legally banned from entering the city until he had formally discharged his duties and celebrated a triumph if one was due. So Sulla was sticking to the rules.[1] Maybe a return to the constitutional *status quo ante bellum* was possible after all.

Sulla had other ideas. He had attempted the forgive and forget approach before, after he had marched on Rome in 88 BC. At that time he had (in his opinion) passed the death sentence on the minimum number of those responsible for illegal legislation and the even more illegal riots, sedition and insurgency that had followed. As a reward for his restraint, Cinna had taken power and Marius had stalked the streets of Rome slaying whomever took his fancy. Sulla had been outlawed, and his friends persecuted, hunted down and executed. Even his wife and family had been in fear of their lives. Very well. This time Sulla would do it differently. Instead of the customary office of proconsul, he would revive the ancient office of dictator, unused for the past 120 years. Then as dictators were appointed to do, he would set Rome to rights. And no one would object, because anyone likely to object would be dead.

As Sulla addressed the senate, there came sounds of confusion from the Villa Publica, a nearby establishment on the Campus Martius. Usually the building was the censors' base of operations in Rome, but the wide space around could hold a large number of people; so here the thousands of Samnite prisoners from the recent battle were being held. Sulla continued to talk calmly as the shouts coming from outside the senate house changed to screams as Sulla's men methodically slaughtered every prisoner. As a signal of intent, nothing could be clearer. Constitutional government had not returned yet to Rome – instead the Romans had exchanged the haphazard Marian killings for the more cold-blooded, thorough and precise purge of Sulla.

The initial bout of murders set the entire city on edge, for no one knew whom Sulla planned to kill and whom he intended to spare. A relative of that Catulus killed by the Marians put the question to Sulla directly. 'So who are we going to live with then, if we kill armed men in wartime, and unarmed men when at peace?'[2] Metellus asked the same question, both as a solid Sullan supporter and perhaps the only decent human still involved in Roman politics. 'Punish those you must,' he urged, 'but at least put out of their uncertainty those whom you have decided to spare.' When Sulla grumpily replied that he had not yet decided whom to spare, Metellus said 'Well at least let us know which persons you are definitely going to punish.'[3]

More or less on the spot, Sulla produced a list of eighty names. These men were to be killed on sight, immediately and without trial. Furthermore, anyone assisting the men so named would automatically append their names to the list by so doing. These totally unlawful execution orders produced widespread indignation at their illegality, and horror at the proposed number of victims. Horror changed to fear the next day when Sulla, after an evening's contemplation, produced a list with a further 220 names, and then again the following day he produced another list with the same number. That was everyone he could remember, Sulla said, but he would add more names if any came to mind. The list of 500 names was called the 'proscription list' – a name that sent shudders down Roman spines even a generation later.

That terrible word – 'proscription'. Of all the mercilessness of Sulla's domination, what cruelty has more been seared into our minds? I believe it is those punishments decreed without trial for men who were Roman citizens.

Cicero, *De domo* 57 BC

Sulla had a long memory. He recalled the legislative and judicial antics of senators and equestrians leading up to the catastrophe of 91 BC. Those equestrians who had terrorized the senate with their dominance of the law courts now experienced the terror of a state with no law courts whatsoever. Anyone who had illegally put to death a supporter of Sulla now experienced the fear of death for himself at first hand. Furthermore, while Sulla seemed purely focused on the twin goals of purging the state and exacting personal revenge, the motives of others were not so pure. Rumours circulated of men first killed for their money, and their names appended to the proscription lists afterwards. When a man with little interest in politics discovered that he had been prescribed, he remarked sardonically, 'Ah. I see my Alban farm has informed on me.' A farm in the Alban hills was a prestige possession among the Roman aristocracy, and demand far exceeded supply – a matter that those 'helping' Sulla with the proscriptions were intent on resolving. This rampant illegality, remarks the historian Velleius Paterculus indignantly, took place in a state where normally an actor could sue for damage to his feelings if he was booed off the stage.[4]

Marius was dead, and his son with him. This left a nephew, Marius Gratidianus who had been among the most bloodthirsty Marians during their time of triumph. He suffered a grisly death, and his corpse was mutilated again thereafter. Lacking Marius himself to kill, Sulla tried to kill his memory. The ashes were disinterred and scattered into the river Anio, and monuments and statues commemorating Marius up and down the country were overthrown and defaced. Overall, it has been estimated that some 5,000 people perished in the proscriptions, though this number does not include those killed collectively as will be seen in the fate of Praeneste and Norba. Furthermore, the general chaos lent itself to extra-curricular killings as wartime grudges were settled and private land grabs took place. (We see an example of the latter, painstakingly described in Cicero's *Pro Roscio Amerino*, in which a young man was accused of murdering his father by the real killers, who had seized his estate.)

Crassus, the hero of the Colline Gate, did much to besmirch his reputation at this time. He had slain family members to avenge, but it was noted that he took his vengeance mostly from those with property he could seize. The particularly egregious killing of a man whose only crime was to have something Crassus wanted finally drew a complaint from Sulla, a man who usually stood by his friends no matter what. Crassus was never employed by Sulla on public business again.

Most of our reports from this period are by Roman aristocrats and those writing for them, so the decimation of the Roman aristocracy attracts much of the interest in our sources. But Sulla's death lists were far beyond individuals. At Praeneste, the garrison surrendered on the younger Marius' death. That Marius' head was already adorning the Roman forum, where Sulla sarcastically quoted a line from the Greek playwright Aristophanes at it: 'first learn to row a ship before you try to steer it'. Now Sulla travelled out to Praeneste to dispose of the rest of the town. Romans, Samnites and natives were divided into separate groups. From among the native people of Praeneste, Sulla picked out those few whom he owed a favour. The rest he had killed along with all the Samnites. The Romans deserved to die as well, Sulla told them, but because they were Romans, he would spare them. The town itself was then comprehensively plundered. Reports of this reached the people of Norba, the fortress guarding the route through the nearby Pomptine marshes. These people too had been holding out against Sulla, and when it was certain the town would fall, the population indulged in an orgy of mutual massacre before setting fire to the place, so that there was little but bones and ashes left for the Sullan army when it took possession. The city of Volterrae in Etruria took note also, and hung on stubbornly until 80 BC until resistance was crushed personally by Sulla in his final military command.

Sulla arbitrarily rearranged matters in municipalities across Italy. Lands were taken from some pro-Marian cities and given to Sulla's soldiers who were settled as something between retirement and a standby reserve in case of trouble. Other cities had their citadels or walls demolished, or had to pay substantial fines (which went to restore the depleted Roman exchequer, as the property and other assets of the proscribed were also properly supposed to do.) While much of Italy suffered from Sulla's wrath, as expected, the people of Samnium took the brunt of it.

Sulla's proscriptions only came to an end when all who called themselves Samnites had been killed or driven from Italy. When asked the reason for his terrible anger, Sulla explained that he had learned from experience that no Roman would ever be safe so long as there were Samnites to deal with. So what were once towns have become villages, and some have vanished altogether. Boeanum, Aesernia, Panna, Venafrum near Telesia, none of them can properly be called towns today.

Strabo, Geography 5.4.11

The name of Aesernia in this list shows how little reward the city received for its valiant defence against the Italian rebels. After its surrender it had become a stronghold for the Samnites and Marians, and when the Sullan army reconquered Aesernia they so devastated the city that it only recovered some of its former size under the emperor Trajan, almost two centuries later.

Death was not the only punishment inflicted by the new regime. Dozens of leading men were exiled, and their sons barred from holding public office. ('Only Sulla could dream up ways of punishing those yet unborn' remarked the later consul Lepidus while in the course of undoing that legislation.[5]) Sulla did not look kindly on disobedience. Ofella, the general who had served Sulla well in maintaining the siege of Praeneste, decided to run for magisterial office despite being firmly told by Sulla that this was out of the question. This was because Ofella was an equestrian, and Sulla was determined to restore at least the appearance of the old constitution. While Ofella publicly put his case to the people in the forum, Sulla had him cut down, and briefly dismissed the murder with the words, 'Know, people of Rome, that this man disobeyed me.' Another who disobeyed Sulla was the young Julius Caesar. He stubbornly remained married to Cornelia, the daughter of the Marian leader Cinna, despite having had strict orders to divorce himself from her. Instead Caesar went on the run. He, like most of those on the wanted list, was quickly captured and only the fact that a number of Sulla's allies were also Caesar's relatives saved the young man from immediate execution. (The couple remained married for another decade until Cornelia's untimely death.)

While Sulla remained organizing matters in Rome and Italy, young Pompey was dispatched to clean up the remnants of Marian resistance in Sicily and

Africa. Pompey conducted himself with great restraint with regard to the general population; going even so far as to have soldiers' swords sealed in their scabbards as a disincentive for untoward behaviour. However, those senior Marians whom Pompey captured (including the ex-consul Carbo) he executed with a grim enthusiasm that earned him the nickname '*carnifex adulescens*' – the young butcher. (No one needed to ask who the 'old butcher' was.) Africa came quickly under Sullan control, but Iberia was to prove more problematic. The junior Marian leader Sertorius came into his own as governor of the peninsula. He proved himself a master at both bringing the local tribes under his control and in deploying them in guerrilla warfare against Sullan armies sent to bring him down. So prolonged and stubborn was Sertorius' resistance that the last of the Marians eventually had the satisfaction of outliving his nemesis, Sulla.

Sulla had taken his revenge, and in the process had systematically removed anyone who might stand in the path of his intended reforms. With Italy cowed and most of the rest of the empire again under Roman control, it was now time set about repairing the damaged country and constitution. Here Sulla seemed determined that the disasters of the past decade would never be repeated. Whatever his personal feelings towards giving citizenship to the Italians, Sulla knew that particular genie could never be put back into the bottle. This was not least because many of the 'Roman' soldiers under his command had been Italians at the start of 91 BC. Now these men were settled on Roman land and enjoying the privileges of Roman law and citizenship. Revoking that citizenship was perhaps the only thing that Sulla could do that would break the fierce loyalty his ex-soldiers felt for him, so Sulla did not even try. Pragmatically, he accepted that most of Italy south of the Alps was either Roman or would soon become so.

It was at this point that Sulla set about formalizing his position. After the election of the consuls for the coming year, the process was started that would officially make Sulla the dictator that he already was in practice. Though Sulla took the ancient name he set a new precedent, for previous dictators had strict terms of reference and limits to their time in office. Sulla's dictatorship was open-ended. Furthermore, the legislation was proposed by the official overseeing the election of the consuls, the *interrex*, in the one and only time in Roman history that this official has ever proposed legislation, let alone a law of such far-reaching significance. The legislation was through a *lex rogata* – that is, by a direct proposal to the people of Rome. This deliberately bypassed the senate, either to absolve that body from involvement, to forestall objections, or to make it seem that Sulla was dictator by popular demand. The same law incidentally gave formal absolution for any extra-legal activities Sulla might have conducted in the past.

There was now the question of the senate. This had been considerably depleted by the Italian war, for whatever the sins of the Roman aristocracy, their courage was undoubted. Senators had served in the front lines throughout the war, and had taken disproportionate casualties. Then, even while senators were still being killed by the Samnites and other Italian hold-outs, there came the ructions of 88 BC. After his march on Rome Sulla killed a handful of senators, including Sulpicius, and thereafter Cinna and Marius killed a good many more when they got back into power. Then when Sulla returned and civil war flared up again, still more senators had perished in the fighting. Then Sulla had conducted his own very strict purge which by itself took out over a hundred senators. Overall, it had not been a good decade for the conscript fathers of the Roman Republic, and since matters had been in disarray, the censors had been slow to replenish the senate's depleted ranks.

Sulla set about not only bringing the senate up to its proper number, but also proposed the addition of three hundred new senators. This was originally the brainchild of Livius Drusus who had intended to bring the equestrian class more into the ranks of government. At the time the senate had rejected that idea with the same vehemence that it had rejected the idea of citizenship for the Italians. Now the measure was accepted with hardly a murmur. Recent years had provided a harsh reality check, and the senate was less prepared to defy reality. Sulla also made official what had long been standard practice – that once a man was voted to magisterial office, he was automatically adlected into the senate. Since the first step in a magisterial career was the quaestorship, Sulla raised the number of quaestors to twenty. This both met the need for junior administrators in Rome's growing empire and appears to reflect the number of senators whom modern estimates of Roman mortality rates indicate would be needed to keep the number stable.

Sulla now turned to the tribunate, the office that he deemed responsible for many of the evils that had afflicted Rome. After all, the Gracchus brothers,

Livius Drusus, and most recently the wretched Sulpicius had caused huge turmoil by 'abusing' the powers of the tribunate, so Sulla was determined to strip the office of its potential for mischief. Stage one was to make the office a dead end rather than a springboard to power. So Sulla arranged it so that a man who had held the tribunate was not eligible for any other magistracy. At a stroke this meant that no Roman with plans for a political career would even consider the job. Also the power of tribunes to propose legislation was severely curtailed – never again would a Sulpicius use his power over the mob to pass laws forcing a legally appointed general to renounce his command. While the tribunes kept their right to save individual citizens from magisterial persecution, their ability to veto legislation was limited to particular circumstances. No future Tiberius Gracchus would use his veto to bring state business to a halt.

In short 'Sulla left the tribunate as an insubstantial shadow of itself'.[6] It seems not to have occurred to Sulla that the tribunes were at their most disruptive when reflecting the needs of the people they represented, and curtailing the powers of the tribunes did not solve the huge social problems to which the tribunes gave a voice. Instead Sulla suppressed even discussion of the very issues which the Roman state most needed to resolve. And suppressing the issues did not make them go away, as demonstrated by the support given by the lower classes to the gladiator uprising of Spartacus less than a decade later. Yet even more crucially, it was the lower classes who made up the backbone of the legions. If they were denied a role in the formal workings of the state, they were certainly able to make their wishes known in an extra-constitutional manner. Caesar, and later Octavian, grasped this point. The odd thing is that Sulla, who used his legions to ride roughshod over the government in Rome, appears not to have drawn the lesson taught by his own actions.

Outside Italy Sulla, thanks to his campaigns against Mithridates, was aware that corruption and misgovernment by Roman governors was not just wrong in itself, but led to oppressed provincials giving whole-hearted support to foreign invaders. Therefore misgovernment was a security issue. Sulla's response was to make provincial governors more answerable to the senate. While in the past provincial governors might be serving praetors or even consuls if there was an expectation of military action in a province, after Sulla there is a noted tendency for provincial government to be left to those consuls and praetors who had already served their year in office. Apart from anything else, this meant that there was someone minding the shop in Rome and could take immediate charge when something like the Mithridatic war broke out. And to make it less likely that such a war would break out, Sulla made misbehaviour by a provincial governor a treasonable offence. This was done by re-working the already existing law on *maiestas* (the crime of 'diminishing the majesty of the Roman people'). A standing court now sat in judgement of governors who crossed the boundaries of their province – especially those who took their army with them. Declarations of war against an ally and the illegal detention of prisoners were also covered, as was the crime of tampering with the loyalty of the army. Sulla did not want anyone repeating his own actions. Regrettably we do not know the full extent of the law and whether it covered peculation by governors within their own province – though doubtless the *repetundae* laws were also re-examined. Our ignorance of the exact provisions of the *Lex Cornelia de maiestas* are partly through gaps in the sources but partly because the provisions of the law were deliberately imprecise. The actual purpose of the law was to allow the senate to act against a governor gone bad, and the provisions of the law were left flexible enough to be adapted to fit the case against the governor in question (or indeed against anyone else the senate happened to be gunning for).[7]

Sulla's constitutional measures are sometimes described as the knee-jerk response of a dyed-in-the-wool conservative determined to hold back the forces of change, and there is some justice in the charge. After all, the Roman state had undergone considerable change in the past ten years, and none for the better. (Apart from the very large exception of citizenship for the Italians, but in Sulla's time the jury was still out on whether this was a good thing.) A closer examination of the record shows that when not being a cold-blooded agent of human extinction Sulla could be both thoughtful and reasonable. His legal reforms are a case in point. It is highly probable that Sulla increased the number of serving praetors from six to eight.[8] While the original job of the praetor had been to command armies when Rome's military commitments made it impossible for the consuls to be everywhere at once, the post-Sullan praetor had his responsibilities in Rome itself. These were both judicial and administrative, and in the latter role took over some of the work of the censors. Unlike other Roman magistracies, censors were not elected every year, and their responsibilities had increased as the Roman state had grown in complexity. Before the Sullan change, a pair of censors could spend their time in office working through an accumulated backlog without ever getting to the business on hand. Now praetors could deal with matters as they arose and, once their year in office was complete, praetors were available – and suitably trained in law and administration – for the running of minor provinces.

We can quickly pass over Sulla's attempts to legislate for public morality. Contemporary Romans saw little point in being lectured on proper behaviour by a man renowned for spendthrift drunken parties with actors and prostitutes, and who didn't even obey his own laws after they were passed. It is, however, worth noting that in later years the serial adulterer Augustus also tried hard to appear as the custodian of public morality. This particular form of hypocrisy is by no means limited to ancient Rome, but one notes that Romans of questionable character were particularly prone to pass moralizing legislation, thus confirming the observation of one ancient writer that 'the more a man lacks ethics, the more he needs laws'.

While his sumptuary legislation quickly became redundant, a more lasting change was Sulla's enlargement of the *pomerium*, the official boundary of the city of Rome. Since the Roman world was divided into Rome, places ruled by Rome and places due to be conquered by Rome, the enlargement of the 'Rome' bit was a very serious business, which involved considerable research and legal and religious rituals. (For example certain temples of foreign gods were not allowed within the *pomerium*, and bodies could only be interred there in exceptional circumstances.) The complexity involved in such enlargements and the conflicting interests of all involved meant that enlargements of the *pomerium* happened seldom, and usually when there was someone like Sulla who had the indisputable final word on disagreements.

Towards the end of 81 BC Sulla began to disengage from autocracy. As a transition he resigned his dictatorship and immediately stood for election as consul for the following year. Sulla campaigned as might any other candidate, greeting potential voters in the forum and cheerfully arguing his case with anyone who called him to account.

He put more trust in his good fortune than in his accomplishments, and although he had slain great numbers of its citizens and introduced numerous changes and innovations to Rome's government, he relinquished the office of dictator and put the selection of consuls into the hands of the electorate. He walked up and down in the forum like a private citizen, exposing his person freely to those who wanted to charge him with his past actions.

Plutarch, *Life of Sulla* 34

Sulla was duly elected with Metellus Pius as his colleague. Then, once his year in office was complete, Sulla retired from public life.

On the face of it, all was well after a tumultuous decade. Rome had overcome the threat of extinction at the hands of rebellious Italians, and peace had returned to the peninsula, with most of the population either content with the prospect of citizenship or (especially in the case of the Samnites) dead. The flaws in the Roman constitution, which had led to an overweening and self-interested senate, had been corrected by making that body more inclusive and more answerable to the public. The threat posed by Mithridates had been, if not quashed, at least forced into dormancy. (A Sullan subordinate called Murena had made a second, quasi-official attempt to attack Pontus but the Roman government swiftly disavowed Murena after his attack failed miserably. The resolution of the Pontic question remained for a future generation.) Sulla himself was happily married to a wife who had just borne him twin children. The future seemed bright – but it wasn't.

Two years after Sulla retired into private life, he was dead. From accounts of his death it seems that a gastric ulcer exacerbated by years of alcohol abuse had become infected. Unnoticed at first, the corruption spread until Sulla almost literally rotted away from within. 'All his clothing, baths, hand-basins and food were tainted with the flood of corruption, so violently did it erupt. He immersed himself many times a day in water to wash away the infection, but in vain. The infestation gained rapidly on him and defied all purification.'[9] Finally, after suffering a violent internal haemorrhage, Sulla died in 78 BC. His illness and death are an appropriate metaphor for the Republic he left behind. That Republic was to last another twenty-nine years, but as with Sulla in 80 BC, despite the outward appearance of health, insidious internal rot had already passed the point of no return.

Epilogue – From Sulla to Caesar

S ulla's reforms had put the state back on an even keel, but he had righted a ship that was already sinking. In the event, few of Sulla's changes to the system were to endure – but then the Roman Republic would not last very much longer either. There were two reasons for the failure of the Roman Republic even after Sulla's attempts to mend its ills. One was psychological and the other was systemic.

The systemic problem with the republic was that it no longer represented its citizens. When every male Roman citizen was also a practising Roman voter, the needs of the people found a voice in the legislature. Likewise when almost every Roman soldier was also a practising Roman voter, the will of the people and the will of the army were pretty much the same thing. However, as the Roman state expanded, an increasing number of 'Romans' lived their lives without even seeing the city of which they were technically citizens. And since all voting by Romans had to be done personally in Rome, this meant that an ever-increasing number of citizens were effectively disenfranchised. This problem resulted in very literal class warfare.

There is a largely discredited idea from the mid-twentieth century that from the time of the Gracchi the Roman state was divided into two political parties. These were the demagogic *populares* and the oligarchic optimates. By this theory, the two parties operated as proto-forms of modern political parties, with assumed manifestos and a rough hierarchy. More recent scholarship has dismissed this idea, pointing out that Roman aristocrats were as individualistic as cats and socially incapable of subsuming their personal ambitions to a larger political organization. The modern opinion is that individual politicians took different routes to power, being *populares* when it seemed expedient to appeal to the people, and optimates when the best option was through the use of friendships and personal connections in the senate. Some politicians favoured one route more than the other, but their choices were dictated more by pragmatism than ideology, and others on the same path were more likely to be considered rivals than brothers-in-arms.

Nevertheless, the *populares* versus optimates theory has some validity. This is because after the Italian war, and despite the efforts of Sulla (himself widely considered an optimate), the constitutional balance of power was decisively tipped in favour of the wealthy. A peasant in the mountains of Umbria could not afford to take a month off to go to Rome and cast his vote on legislation that nobody had bothered to inform him about in the first place. However, the wealthy landowner next door would be well up to speed on proposed legislation that affected his interests, and had the means to go to Rome and the connections and money to influence the vote in his favour when he got there. So legislation tended to favour the wealthy and well-connected. The poor of Italy lacked political sophistication, and it is doubtful whether our theoretical Umbrian peasant would have been able to articulate the problems with the system that stopped him from getting a fair shake, but it is clear that a great many of those in Italy knew that the system was not working in their favour.

This is one of the major causes of the unrest in the countryside between the time of Sulla and Caesar. Almost as soon as Sulla was dead, the consul Lepidus sought to overturn much of Sulla's constitutional handiwork. Rebuffed in Rome, he took his cause to the country and above all to the army. Soon afterwards Spartacus and his gladiators led a rebellion. The nihilist style of the uprising had a visceral appeal for the lower classes – there were probably at least as many of the free poor in Spartacus' army as gladiators or escaped slaves, and Spartacus had literally to turn away more volunteers. This popular endorsement of a man whose cause consisted almost entirely of pillage and rapine was a symptom that the Roman social order lacked grass-roots support. Even Sulla's veterans, once established on the land, found that the system was not designed to favour smallholders. This, added to the fact that many ex-soldiers did not take naturally to farming in the first place, made Sulla's veterans natural recruits for seditiously minded individuals such as Catiline in the sixties.

But perhaps the most resounding condemnation of the post-Sullan system came when Caesar crossed the Rubicon in 49 BC. By this time Pompey was a senior statesman and the military leader of the Roman senatorial party. He had boasted, 'If I stamp my foot, Italy will rise.' But when it came to the crunch and Pompey needed the support of the Italian people, Italy didn't rise. It yawned. The people of Italy were simply not vested in the system as it stood. Few saw much benefit in taking the side of one aristocrat or another in a senatorial squabble that was only going to make everyone's life worse no matter how it turned out. Thus we see one aspect of the systemic problem in Italy – the disenfranchisement and subsequent alienation of the poor. The second aspect of this disenfranchisement was that though they had almost completely lost their representation in formal politics, this certainly did not mean that the poor lost their ability to influence events. If the *dominiatio Sullae* had taught anything, it was that the sword was mightier than the constitution, and the men wielding those swords were the very men who were no longer represented in the formal political process – the common people of Italy.

Again, the enfranchisement of the Italian peoples came too late to solve the problem, and in fact exacerbated it. For not only were the legions of Pompey, Caesar and Octavian packed with men who had never voted in Rome, many of those men had relatives who had very recently fought against Rome, if indeed they had not been on the opposite side themselves. Such men had little inhibition about supporting a general who claimed to represent their interests in a way that the senate and Roman voters could not, or would not, do.

The most significant of these interests lay in what happened to a Roman soldier after he was discharged. In the early Republic, a peasant living close to Rome would simply report for the seasonal campaign and return to his smallholding after the season was over, probably taking time to vote in the annual elections *en route*. After the Marian reforms, the property qualification for membership of the legions was waived. When stood down (which now might be after up to a decade serving under the standards in Iberian or Asia Minor) these soldiers had nowhere to go, and a skill set incompatible with most civilian careers, since it basically involved being very good at killing people. With little faith in the senate or government, these men looked to their general to provide them with a smallholding, preferably in Italy, from which they could support themselves at the end of what now amounted to a military career. And whatever the general said that his men needed to do to get their pensions, the legionaries were quite prepared to do. As with the other common people of Italy, they had little interest in supporting a senate and constitution that did not support them.

Thus the major changes of the decade 91–81 BC came too late to repair the damaged fabric of Roman political life, and instead the manner in which those changes came about meant that there were now even more Romans to be disenchanted with Roman governance than before, and more Romans to serve under military commanders whose own commitment to the political system was suspect(see below). The systemic flaws in the Roman state had, if anything, been expanded rather than fixed by the violent convulsions of the decade.

And then there was the psychological aspect. A government that had been blatantly used as the tool of a self-interested aristocracy in the years up to 91 BC was hardly going to inspire faith in the system. Then, after the Italian war erupted as a direct result of the incompetence of the oligarchic government in power, this war became subsumed into a civil war fought between Roman aristocrats with motives which were hardly inspiring to the average citizen. Yes, Sulla had been displaced from command of his army but 'put Sulla back in charge of the Mithridatic war' was hardly a slogan to die for. In fact the absence of a compelling ideology on either side of the Marian/Sullan conflict was one of the distinguishing features of the war.

Sulla's men had a clear idea of what they were fighting for – a general they believed in, and the chance of a decent post-campaign settlement for themselves. Those in the ranks of the army opposing Sulla lacked a compelling reason why they should be there. After Marius' arbitrary executions in Rome, and the cheerful disregard of all sides for once-venerated constitutional conventions, the idea that the Marians represented liberty against Sullan tyranny was a tough one to sell. And while Censorinus might really not like Crassus, this was not a compelling reason to die for Censorinus. Hence the massive desertions that were a feature of the war against Sulla. Men deserted because they had nothing to fight for. The exception was the Samnites and Lucanians. They saw clearly that they were fighting for their freedom, their homeland and their very lives. And so they fought, fought well and came very close to winning. If all Italy had been similarly motivated, Sulla would not have made it past Brundisium.

But in fact claims that the Marians represented proper, legitimate government were so weak that few writers, modern or contemporary, bother mentioning them. Certainly Sulla was brutal to his opponents (as were the Marians in their less organized way) but the Sullan war was a vendetta among the aristocracy that had little to do with liberty versus autocracy. The basic fact was that outside the Roman senate and equestrian class there was precious little liberty going about. Writers on the early empire were wont to lament the 'loss' of Republican freedoms. Yet the senate and equestrians did not share that freedom with their fellow Romans, nor with the Italians and certainly not with the provincials. Almost without exception every part of Italy was better off under the rule of the Caesars than it was in the last century of the Republic. As to whether the people of Italy lost their freedom under the imperial autocracy, well, perhaps the ghosts of Fregellae are best placed to answer that.

Thus we see that the common people of Italy were largely shut out of the constitutional process but very dynamically involved in the extra-constitutional events that so enlivened the last years of the Roman Republic. We now turn to the leaders of the post-Sullan state, which was once again the aristocracy, albeit an aristocracy in which the Roman element was much depleted and the Italian element greatly expanded. The *domi nobiles* – the rural aristocracy of Italy – were now to play an ever-increasing role in Roman politics, as demonstrated by the career of one of the fore-runners; the consul of 63 BC, Marcus Tullius Cicero of Arpinum. However, the leadership in Rome had been as damaged by the events of 91–81 BC as had the people of Italy. This was not simply in the appalling attrition suffered by senatorial families over the decade. Casualties in the Hannibalic war of the third century had been at least as high, and the Roman state and aristocracy had rebounded strongly from this. The issue lay in the manner that these casualties had been inflicted.

The Italian war was damaging enough – in this war the Roman fought countrymen with whom they shared ties of marriage, commerce and friendship. Furthermore, it was clear to everyone from the beginning that this war was a self-inflicted injury caused by self-interest and short-sighted politics. Consequently the damage wrought by this war had both an apparent side and an insidious one. Firstly, it introduced the idea of resolving internal political questions by military force. This was not how issues had been previously resolved within the Roman state, and technically it was not what happened in the Italian war, because the Italians were not Romans – but as mentioned above, they were close enough that it almost counted, so the idea was introduced.

With the idea established, it followed naturally that Sulla should use military force to resolve the issue of 'mob anarchy' in Rome, and that those in Rome should try to organize a military response to Sulla. Then, when the Marians re-took Rome after Sulla's departure for the east, this was yet another extension of military force into the area of political disagreement. Nor was it hard to notice that the military force became more extreme and extra-constitutional with every application. By the time that Sulla returned, the use of force to compel political submission was so established that Sulla fought almost a standard campaign of conquest not much different from that by which he had extracted Greece from the clutches of Mithridates. As military force became a recognized means of gaining political power, constitutional conventions suffered accordingly. Things that would have been unimaginable in 91 BC were standard practice a decade later. This meant not only irregularities such as the younger Marius being made consul although totally unqualified for the job, or Sulla being made dictator in a novel manner with unprecedented terms of reference. It was also matters such as an elected consul (Octavius) being lynched in the forum when the opposing faction took the city, another elected consul (Carbo) being summarily executed by Pompey in Sicily, and the head of another consul (the younger Marius) being placed on a pike in the forum for the edification of the voters.

In these and numerous other ways, the Roman constitution, once a venerated instrument of state, became an increasingly ignored irrelevance. Not just the younger Marius but many of his elder contemporaries finished their political careers upon pikes. For the post-Sullan generation, the effect of seeing their fathers, uncles and other kinsmen so displayed cannot but have undermined faith in the political process. What we see in the last generation of the Roman Republic – cynical abuse of governmental and religious institutions, a readiness to resort to violence and a grim determination to win at all costs – are features that were always present in the Roman character but magnified out of all proportion by the traumas of 91–81 BC. The Roman aristocracy no longer believed that the state or the constitution could protect them or their families. How could they when they had seen such dramatic proof to the contrary?

Before 91 BC, a political resolution of Italy's problems was achievable. Drusus and his predecessors pushed hard for such a resolution and despite occasional outbreaks of violence, the struggle for reform was largely through constitutional means. In fact it was those opposed to reform who were first and readiest to resort to violence when they felt their interests were threatened. Even so, the Italians pressed their case in the legislature and senate for decades before they eventually turned to armed rebellion. If the Roman Republic had suffered from a sudden attack of statesmanship and brought the Italians gradually and peacefully into the body of the Roman state, this would have set a precedent. The resolution of other major issues, such as the alienation of the army, might also have been peacefully managed.

Let it not be forgotten that the Roman state had already achieved one conceptual breakthrough in the hitherto unthinkable idea that a man could be a citizen of one city while permanently domiciled and active in the politics of another. Given goodwill on all sides, something approximating representational government through senators from different regions was entirely possible. At least, possible before 91–81 BC. That calamitous decade destroyed the faith of the people of Italy not just in the senate and Roman government (as there was little faith there to begin with), but in negotiation and the political process as a whole.

That disastrous time left the post-Sullan generation of aristocrats with a grimmer and more cynical outlook, and they were much readier to believe that change, or the prevention of change, could only be achieved by naked force – within or without the constitution. This is why in 49 BC the senate was prepared to violate the constitution and over-ride a tribunican veto in order to bring down Caesar, and why Caesar was prepared to ignore the constitution and march on Rome allegedly in defence of tribune's rights. That sequence of events marked not just the final collapse of the Roman Republic, but proof that the Republic had been unsalvageable for decades. The Republic did not collapse because Caesar crossed the Rubicon. It collapsed because nobody believed in it any more.

FINIS

Notes

Chapter 1
1. 'Hybrida' meant a Roman of Spanish stock.
2. Lucilius as quoted in *Fragments of Old Latin* Loeb University Press. 5.14.
3. Plutarch, C. Gracch 12.

Chapter 2
1. Sallust, *Jugurthine War* 35.
2. Sallust, *Jugurthine War* 40.
3. This Julia was the aunt of the Julius Caesar famous for later overthrowing the Roman Republic.
4. Plutarch, *Marius* 7.
5. Ibid. 8.
6. Plutarch, *Sulla* 2.
7. Ibid. 4.

Chapter 3
1. *Cambridge Ancient History IX.* S.A. Cook, F.E. Adcock, M.P. Charlesworth eds.
2. In De officiis 3.47.
3. Appian, BC 1.46.
4. This was not true of some of the earliest maritime colonies. These coastal settlements were designed to deter piracy and the inhabitants were expected to remain *in situ*.
5. e.g. Varro, *De Lingua Latine* 5.143.

Chapter 4
1. As an aside, this Drusus was probably the grandfather of Livia, wife of Augustus, just as Rutilius Rufus was Julius Caesar's great-uncle. The Roman senatorial class were a very close-knit group.
2. In the words of Velleius Paterculus, *History* 2.13.
3. *De viris illustribus* 66.
4. Alternatively it may have been their Roman citizenship that would not stand scrutiny, as some frustrated Italians had taken to unilaterally awarding themselves citizenship, and the Roman authorities were cracking down on this.
5. The incident is related in Diodorus Siculus 37.13.

6. Pliny, *Natural History* 33.3.46. The 'Livius Drusus' Pliny refers to may have been the father of our Drusus, but the son seems much more likely a candidate.
7. *De viris illustribus* 66.
8. Obsequens, *Prodigies* 114. (54).

Chapter 5
1. His immediate ancestors included Decius Magius, a highly pro-Roman citizen of Capua during the Hannibalic War whose namesake was deeply involved in the war of 90 BC.
2. Smiths *Dictionary of Greek and Roman Biography* p. 3158.
3. Plutarch, *Life of Sulla* 6.
4. Appian, BC 1.38 says that this Caepio was the former consul now administering the area, but this seems to have been Appian confusing both his Servilii Caepiones and the administrative system in 91 BC.
5. Diod. 37.13.
6. Exactly which tribes rebelled and when is a matter of continuing controversy. Here I present a synthesis of modern research and a resolution of confusing and contradictory ancient evidence rather than a definite list.
7. *Epitome* of Livy 72.

Chapter 6
1. Appian, BC 1.37.
2. Asconius 74.
3. As with the tribes in revolt, the question of which Italian generals were in command and when is unclear and controversial.
4. Cic., *Pro Fonteio* 43.
5. Dio 29.98.
6. Cic., *De leg. Agr.* 2.80.
7. Frontinus Stratagems 2.4.16.
8. Appian, BC 1.42.
9. At least Appian says it was Sextus, but he might have confused his Caesars for the context works better if he meant the consul Lucius.
10. Appian, 1.43.
11. Dio fr 98.3.
12. Orosius, *Contra Pag.* 5.18.
13. The feast day of the Magna Matua was the Materalia of 11 June on which day married women offered cakes baked in clay pots to the Goddess.

Chapter 7
1. *Periochae* 73.5.
2. Plutarch, *Life of Marius* 33.
3. Orosius 5.18.
4. Appian in BC 1.48 also maintains that this Caesar died while besieging Asculum, which is improbable.

5. This man is sometimes called Judacilius in other sources.
6. Appian, BC 1.48.
7. Ibid. 1.49.
8. Macrobius, *Saturnalia* 1.11.24.
9. Plutarch, *Life of Sulla* 6.

Chapter 8
1. Plutarch, *Life of Marius* 31.
2. Valerius Maximus 11.4.2 and Plutarch, *Life of Sulla* 24.4. respectively.
3. Appian, *Mithridatica* 23.
4. Diod. 37.2.11.
5. Though not into the tribe Pollio, because for reasons we need not go into here, this tribe was too large already.
6. *Cf* the more detailed argument by Salmon 1958.
7. Plutarch, *Life of Marius* 34.
8. Appian, BC 1.57.
9. Appian, BC 1.68.
10. Plutarch, *Life of Marius* 44.
11. Ibid.

Chapter 9
1. Memnnon fr 24 J and Plutarch, *Life of Sulla* 24.
2. Lucullus was almost certainly that quaestor who remained with Sulla on his march on Rome, though definite proof is lacking.
3. Who these men are is uncertain. Metellus was in Africa, Crassus was in Iberia, Pompey in Picenum, and Lucullus had been with Sulla throughout. Thus none of the leaders of the later Sullani could have been among those who fled to Sulla in Greece.
4. Val Max, *Vir ill* 69.4.
5. Badian, 'Waiting for Sulla'.
6. Obsequens *Prodigies* 57.
7. Appian, BC 1.85.
8. Vell. Pat. 2.15.
9. Where his subsequent career is recorded in *Sertorius and the struggle for Spain*, Matyszak, Pen & Sword 2013.
10. Plutarch, *Life of Sulla* 25.
11. Ibid. 28.
12. Appian 1.87, Florus 2.9.23.
13. Appian, BC 1.87.
14. Ibid. 1.89.
15. Ibid. 1.89.
16. Plutarch, *Life of Sulla* 29.
17. Appian, BC 1.93.
18. Vell Pat 2.27.

Chapter 10

1. Even on his visit to Rome earlier in the year, we only hear of Sulla at the Campus Martius, likewise outside the city boundary.
2. *Contra pag.* Orosius 5.21.
3. Plutarch, *Life of Sulla* 31.
4. Vel Pat 2.28.
5. Sallust *hist* 1.55.6M.
6. Vell Pat 2.30.
7. cf Colunga 2011, *Journal Jurispudence.*
8. There is no record for him doing this, but there were six praetors before Sulla's time and eight are attested thereafter, so the logical presumption is that Sulla is responsible for the change.
9. Plut. Sull. 36.

Index